Every Day With Jesus

Victor C. Speakman

Design and Layout:

Authentic Living Publishing

ISBN: 978-0-9759263-8-3

All Scriptures are Notated from
The King James Version

...

DEDICATION

I dedicate this devotional to my father Bishop AC Speakman, a remarkable leader and visionary in both faith and business. Your unwavering guidance, wisdom, and strength have shaped not only my life but the lives of many others who have been fortunate enough to know you.

As a cannon in business, you have set a standard of excellence and integrity that inspires all who work alongside you. Your entrepreneurial spirit and dedication to success have left an indelible mark on the world.

As a great leader in faith, your compassion, wisdom, and unwavering faith have touched the hearts of countless individuals. Your commitment to serving others and spreading the message of love and hope has made a lasting impact on the community.

Thank you, for being a shining example of leadership, faith, and perseverance. Your legacy will continue to inspire and guide us for generations to come.

FOREWORD

Racing through the halls of East Orange General Hospital, a baby voice is heard, little peeping eyes, head full of hair baby child rushed from the dark as if to say, "hello world I have something important to share with you." Finding my joy at that moment did not easily materialize. Today, I am a proud and thankful Mother Velma L. Speakman of a dedicated, writer, teacher, preacher, singer, pastor, and a friend.

My youngest son Victor a "man of valor" has taken me to another level of gratitude and appreciation for a dynamic man whose life has taken different turns but all the while the Lord opened Victor's mouth on that day of his birth, he was born to prepare and to declare the Glory of God to everyone he can reach. Writing great books to encourage people has been a serious love of his and to demonstrate a life that is committed to the cause of Christ takes precedence over some other things he enjoys. Victor remains dedicated to his God given assignments.

Victor was awarded as an "All State Recipient" through the late Mrs. Carolyn Nephew, Director of Music at Gordan High School in Decatur, GA, for the melodious tenor voice which is recognized when he speaks. Unmistaken as he reads the Bible through with readers who tune in to listen and follow along.

Victor prepares daily illuminating messages for readers who seek help growing, this devotional lifts us and encourage us while gaining strength, insight and wisdom from the powerful enlightening Word of God that brings clarity and insight to live and grow by each day. Never boasting but is the first to salute many whose lives have launched them to heights untold. Some have declared victory because of the great truth shared with them, they too are 'living for Jesus a life that is true, striving to please Him in all that they do."

This young man is helping others to get the Word out "Jesus Saves, heals, sets-free, delivers, blesses, lifts, walks with us, talks with us, abides in us, and promises never to leave us." No better hope is described in the pages of a devotional like this that will bring a smile to your face and put a bounce in your step. I challenge you to focus on improving your outlook by reading daily this powerful devotional.

Unbuckle your seat belts, relax in the comfort of your surroundings, and just allow yourself to feel the presence of God as your blessings flow through the pages of this magnificent devotional.

Yours In Christ Service,

Velma L. Speakman, Th.D.

Mom

PREFACE

Having a bachelor's in political science and a master's in administrative management, after graduating from seminary, I decided to become even more diverse in my academic pursuits. I opted to pursue a PhD in political science rather than stay on the religious track, suggested, and questioned by some, by not pursuing a traditional PhD in theology or a Doctor of Ministry degree. I believed that these credentials would provide me with quite a diverse outlook on the world and insight both into my church community and the politics shaping the Black church and its connection to the state. My exposure to the late James Cone, Cornel West, Albert Raboteau, and Michael Eric Dyson, to name a few authors, helped to charter my need to explore the intersection of religion and politics both historically and socially. In my attempt to stay centered by not overly emphasizing either the religious or the political, my centeredness is the result of my devotional time…the time I spend with the Lord.

This notion of separation between church and state can sometimes become overwhelming seeing the world as black or white pushing you to a strict religious perspective or a more otherworldly perspective only marginally incorporating your Christian worldview into your daily life. Choosing to go the academic route through teaching with stops along the way in vocational pastoring rather than a strict church-centered pastoral ministry has served me well in shaping my perspective on ministry. While my commitment to my God and faith have not waned, sometimes getting back to the place where I find the necessary support that completes me can be distant. These are the times when daily devotionals can assist in maintaining the presence of the divine while connecting to the world around you. I do not mean just knowing and quoting scripture or just remembering the religious quotes, but making a connection with a perspective that inspires you to a greater sense of selfless fulfillment and your selfless devotion to God for community service.

For nearly twenty years, Pastor Victor Speakman and I had an intimate, somewhat casual, and structured relationship. As an associate minister at, in those days, the church where we attended was called the *House of God Original Free Will Baptist Church* renamed *Bethel Original Free Will Baptist Church*, I had casual interactions with Victor and his three siblings – Shanise, Vincent, and Vernon. At that time, other than Victor's father, Pastor A. C. Speakman, my most significant relationship was with one of his older and now-deceased siblings Vernon. As the years have passed and

Victor and I have matured, our paths have crossed more significantly over the last twenty in our ministerial roles. After graduating high school, he took on a more significant step in ministry, first going to Bible College to prepare him for the total task of coming to his ministerial calling. Next, he became the co/assistant pastor with his father. Then, much later becoming pastor of Bethel after the passing of his father. In the early years, while not the official youth pastor, I did quite a bit of work with the youth department at Bethel with the various trips to the Original Free Will Baptist Youth Conventions in North Carolina, Maryland, New Jersey, and Georgia. While engaging Victor only occasionally as a youth, he was quite present and active in the youth department.

As our paths have converged more significantly over the years, I have seen Victor's growth in ministry the struggles of being a pastor, and his involvement in the *Original Free Will Baptist* organization. He has shared with me his struggles with pastoring and the challenges of personal doctrinal positions associated with organizational support for the *Original Free Will Baptist*. We have engaged in conversation about what I suspect is the content of this devotional exercise. Pastor Speakman has shared with me his perspective on the church where he pastors what he perceives as his legacy and the mark that legacy will have not only on the congregation that he oversees but both the organization that he has been so much a part of all of his life and the Christian community in general. Along with the challenges of ministry, family, and his health, they have contributed to a life that supports the message of this devotional regarding spending daily time with our Lord Jesus.

As a former pastor and member of several institutional church communities, I can attest to the daily challenges of pulling the ropes together to connect between the local church and the community it serves and the obligational support for the other institutions. On most days there are not enough hands to hold all the roles in place. As such, leaning on the guidance of God to sustain you in those moments is the only solution to making the rope long enough, tight enough, and strong enough to keep life's struggles from unraveling is the only solution. In those times, you need to have time to go to a secret place, your secret closet, to both talk to God and hear God's voice. Your personal devotion time is what can keep the ropes together.

I believe that Pastor Speakman's devotional will provide you with an inspirational message that will challenge you to spend time with God in a more intimate way. Also, I believe that the message will bring you into the presence of the sustaining grace of God's hand in your life as a believer. Moreover, this devotional does not promise to be a panacea for your troubles or health, but it does promise to assist you as you walk daily through life's obstacles. Finally, as the mediator between God and man, I believe that this devotional will give you a sense of peace as you walk daily with Jesus.

Peace,

Minister Douglas E. Ealey, M.A., MDiv., PhD

"Our response to God ought to be louder than our request of God" (Unknown).

ACKNOWLEDGMENTS

I am deeply grateful to the following individuals and organizations whose support and encouragement have been instrumental in the creation of this book: Mom: Your unwavering support and love have been my rock all my life. I am grateful for your guidance and belief in me. LaShanta: Your love, patience, and understanding have been my anchor. I am grateful for your constant support and belief in me. Jessica: You are my shining star and will always be my Cookie, Love you.

Bethel: Thank you for entrusting me with the opportunity to lead you as your Senior Pastor for 12 years. Your faith in me has been a source of strength and inspiration.

Dr. Ealey: Thank you for your friendship, wisdom, and unwavering support throughout this journey. Your presence has been a blessing. Gloria, Sheneece, and the Pastor's aid staff: Your support and dedication have been invaluable. Thank you for standing by me and for your unwavering commitment.

Paulette, Hope (Cee Cee) Caldwell, and Sis. Junita: Your support during a challenging time has meant the world to me. I am grateful for your kindness and solidarity. I thank you for having my back while trying to feed the community.

To all that makeup the church of the Living God that will take this book and treasure it for years to come. I simply say thank you.

Day 1

Luke 4:2 Being forty days tempted of the devil. And in those days, he did eat nothing: and when they were ended, he afterward hungered.

Thought: Jesus was Tempted; So, Will You.

Focus: Your Victory Is in The Word

Jesus was led by the Spirit into the wilderness. It was there for forty days that the devil tempted him. The Lord's response to each attack came from God's Word. He did not enter a debate, he simply responded with what was written.

No one is excused from the attacks of the devil. Through temptations and warnings, he will seek to cause you to compromise. Your only defense is the Word of God. You need not enter a debate, simply declare God's Word and remain in His will. Your victory is in the Word.

Day 2

Luke 5:18-19 And, behold, men brought in a bed a man which was taken with a palsy: and they sought means to bring him in, and to lay him before him. And when they could not find by what way they might bring him in because of the multitude, they went upon the housetop, and let him down through the tiling with his couch into the midst before Jesus.

Thought: Faith Will Find A Way

Focus: Your Faith Can Bless Another

While endeavoring to bring a man suffering with the palsy to Jesus, a group of men found no way to enter the house where he was. Refusing to accept defeat, they went to the rooftop, cut a hole in the ceiling, and let him down to Jesus. Their faith found a way. The man was healed.

What is your level of faith? Do you realize that your faith can impact the lives of others? As the Lord leads you into action, let nothing stop you. Your faith has the power to not only bless you but has the power to impact others. Your faith can find a way.

Day 3

Psalm 18:6 In my distress I called upon the Lord, and cried unto my God: he heard my voice out of his temple, and my cry came before him, even into his ears.

Thought: In Times od Distress, Cry To The One That Can Help

Focus: God's Ears Are Open To Your Cry

Where does one turn in times of distress? There is one that has the power to bring peace to your situation. Yes, God has that power and His ears are open to the cries of His children. Why turn to those that neither can help or care enough to respond? Cry unto the Lord, He will respond.

As you find yourself in distress, you can give up, complain to those that have no power to help, or let your cries go before God. His ears are open to your petitions and He has the power to bring deliverance. Cry to the one that will respond.

Day 4

Isaiah 38:1-2 In those days was Hezekiah sick unto death. And Isaiah the prophet the son of Amoz came unto him, and said unto him, Thus saith the LORD, Set thine house in order: for thou shalt die, and not live. Then Hezekiah turned his face toward the wall, and prayed unto the LORD

Thought: Every No Does Not Have To Be Accepted

Focus: Turn Your Face To The Wall And Weep

Hezekiah was told by the prophet to put his house in order. God has sent the message that he would not be healed, he was going to die. Hezekiah knew not to complain to the prophet, he turned his face to the wall and wept before God. The Lord responded and added fifteen years to his life.

No can be a hard answer to accept, especially when sent from God. When it is not acceptable, place your focus on the only one that can help. Turn your face to the wall and weep before God. He alone has the power to correct your situation.

Day 5

1 Corinthians 10:13 There hath no temptation taken you but such as is common to man: but God is faithful, who will not suffer you to be tempted above that ye are able; but will with the temptation also make a way to escape, that ye may be able to bear it.

Thought: Temptation: No One Is Exempt

Focus: God Has Already Made A Way Of Escape

Though growth and maturity takes place, we are never exempt from temptation. We have the joy of knowing that with the temptation, God has already made a way of escape. The enemy will seek to have us believe there is no solution for our situation, but knowing what God has done, we are able to bear it. We are coming out victorious.

There will be times when you will find yourself in challenging situations. The tempter will suggest that only with compromise will you be able to make it. It is essential that you realize that with the temptation, God has already made a way of escape. Cast not away your confidence, you are coming out victorious.

Day 6

Proverbs 9:9 Give instruction to a wise man, and he will be yet wiser: teach a just man, and he will increase in learning.

Thought: Wisdom Joyfully Receives Instruction

Focus: There Is Yet Much to Learn

It is the wise person that gladly receives instruction. Realizing that no one has total knowledge, they gladly accept counsel and information from others. They know that there is yet much to learn. Their wisdom opens the door for further growth.

You have been blessed to learn much. In acknowledging all that you have received, there is yet much more to learn. As a person of wisdom be quick to receive instruction. What you have not yet acquired, others are there to provide. It is a wise man that desires to become wiser.

Day 7

Proverbs 1:28 Then shall they call upon me, but I will not answer; they shall seek me early, but they shall not find me.

Thought: Don't Wait Until It Is Too Late

Focus: Now Is The Time To Call

The Lord continuously calls out to all that they might follow Him. Although He is long-suffering, there comes a time when He will no longer respond. The message is clear, don't wait until it is too late, call now while He answers.

There were times in the history of Israel that they ignored the call of God. Solomon cautioned them regarding what the results could be. It is essential that we do not make that mistake. Tomorrow is not the time to call. Seek Him today while He may be found. Don't wait until it is too late.

Day 8

Proverb 16:20 He that handleth a matter wisely shall find good: and whoso trusteth in the LORD, happy is he.

Thought: Seek God's Counsel Before Taking Action

Focus: He Knows What You Don't

Rushing into deciding, without consulting the Lord, can lead to disappointment. Those that use wisdom, first consult Him. Their results bring them contentment. They have found "good."

How often have you, without consulting the Lord, rushed into making a decision? Unfortunately, you have not demonstrated wisdom. As you learn to seek Him first, you will discover results that bring joy. He knows what you don't.

Day 9

Philippians 2:12 Wherefore, my beloved, as ye have always obeyed, not as in my presence only, but now much more in my absence, work out your own salvation with fear and trembling,

Thought: Obedience To God Is An Everyday Thing

Focus: God Is The Source Of Your Strength

Paul, in his letter to those at Philippi, reminds them of the importance of their obedience to god. He highlights that it cannot only be in his presence that they obey, but even the more in his absence. With a total commitment, they must give themselves to the lord. He is the source of his strength.

Respect, and obedience, to leadership is a part of the life of the believer, but it cannot replace the need to stay focused on the lord. Do not act in obedience simply to please man. With a total commitment, stay true to the one that deserves all honor. When others are looking, and when they are not, remain obedient to god.

Day 10

Joshua 24:14 Now therefore fear the lord, and serve him in sincerity and in truth: and put away the gods which your fathers served on the other side of the flood, and in Egypt; and serve ye the lord.

Thought: God's Criteria To Serve: Sincerity And Truth

Focus: There Can Only Be One God In Your Life

As Joshua spoke to the people of Israel, he reminded them of all that god had done on their behalf. The battles that he fought for them, and the land that he had given them, spoke loudly of his love for them. It was now time for them, with sincerity and truth, to serve him. There could be only one god in their lives.

Surely God has been gracious unto you. The notable miracles that you have received declare both his love for you as well as his ability to bless. You must not allow anything or anyone else to compete with him. You must, in sincerity and truth, worship the true and living God. There can only be one God in your life.

Day 11

Daniel 6:10 Now when Daniel knew that the writing was signed, he went into his house; and his windows being open in his chamber toward Jerusalem, he kneeled upon his knees three times a day, and prayed, and gave thanks before his god, as he did aforetime.

Thought: Let Nothing Stop Your Prayer

Focus: As You Pray Give Thanks

Knowing Daniel's commitment to prayer, the princes and presidents of the kingdom encouraged the King to sign a petition forbidding any one to make a petition other than to King Darius. The punishment was to be placed into the Lion's Den. Once learning that the law was signed, Daniel went into his house, with his windows open, faced Jerusalem and prayed to his God. As he prayed, he gave thanks. He let nothing stop his prayer or his praise.

Your prayer life is essential. You cannot allow anything to stop you from seeking the Lord from a position of confidence. Your prayers must be consistent and offered with thanksgiving. He will respond.

Day 12

2 Kings 4:22-23 And she called unto her husband, and said, send me, I pray thee, one of the young men, and one of the asses, that I may run to the man of God, and come again. And he said, wherefore wilt thou go to him to day? It is neither new moon, nor sabbath. And she said, it shall be well.

Thought: Even Now, God Is Able

Focus: It Shall Be Well

Upon realizing her son, who had suffered a blow to his head had died, his mother requested her husband provide someone to take her to see the man of God. He asked, not knowing his son's condition, why was she going? She answered, "it shall be well". Her faith assured her that her son would be healed.

You will face occurrences where there appears to be no hope. In the midst of those times, listen carefully to the spirit of the Lord. As he directs your actions, follow suit with confidence. It shall be well.

Day 13

Psalm 23:6 Surely goodness and mercy shall follow me all the days of my life.

Thought: You Are Not Walking Alone

Focus: His Goodness And Mercy

David knew what it felt like to experience challenges. His life, on multiple occasions, was threatened. He certainly, at those times, could have wrestled with his emotions. His knowledge of god provided him the victory. He declared, "goodness and mercy shall follow me all the days of my life". He knew that he was never alone.

You will face challenging times. Some will be strong enough to cause you to wonder if you are walking alone. Though your emotions may suggest that, you are never alone. If you carefully look, you will see that goodness and mercy are with you. God will never leave you alone.

Day 14

Luke 6:35 But love ye your enemies, and do good, and lend, hoping for nothing again; and your reward shall be great, and ye shall be the children of the highest: for he is kind unto the unthankful and to the evil.

Thought: Love Others As God Loves Us

Focus: Your Goodness Can Overcome Evil

Jesus challenged his listeners to reach beyond their past responses. They were told to love not simply their friends, but also their enemies. They were to lend, not looking to receive back. They were to maintain kindness to the unthankful, knowing that their goodness would overcome evil.

The world teaches to protect oneself, to love only those that love back, to lend with the expectation to receive. When you became a follower of Jesus, all that changes. Knowing that goodness has the power to overcome evil, love as God loves you. The results will speak for themselves.

Day 15

Acts 3:6 Then Peter said, silver and gold have I none; but such as I have give I thee: in the name of Jesus Christ of Nazareth rise up and walk.

Thought: You Have What People Need

Focus: You Have The Power To Change Lives

On their way to the Temple for prayer, Peter and John connected with a man who was begging alms. Peter initiated a conversation with the man explaining that though he did not have silver or gold, he had what the man needed. Through the power of his prayer, Peter spoke healing into the man's life directing him to rise up and walk. He had exactly what the man needed.

Your prayer life is not simply to receive things; it has given you the power to change lives. Your prayer life has connected you with the Lord, allowing the anointing of God to flow through you. You have been equipped to speak deliverance into the lives of others. You are able to change lives.

Day 16

Acts 1:4 And, being assembled together with them, commanded them that they should not depart from Jerusalem, but wait for the promise of the Father, which, saith he, ye have heard of me.

Thought: Position Yourself To Receive

Focus: God Has Something Needed For Your Journey

As Jesus was about to ascend to his Father, he instructed his disciples to go to Jerusalem and wait. Their obedience was essential. The journey that was before them would require them to receive the promise of the Father. They were not to depart until the promise was fulfilled.

You have been chosen by the Lord to serve Him. Your journey will bring you many challenges for which you will need to be empowered. Position yourself both physically and spiritually, that you might receive the promise of the Father. He will equip you with what is needed for victory.

Day 17

1 Peter 1:14-16 As obedient children, not fashioning yourselves according to the former lusts in your ignorance: But as he which hath called you is holy, so be ye holy in all manner of conversation; Because it is written, Be ye holy; for I am holy.

Thought: In Obedience; We Are To Walk Holy

Focus: A Holy God Has Holy Followers

Peter reminds us that who we were yesterday cannot be who we are today. With a spirit of obedience, now being aware of the lusts that drove us yesterday, we are to walk holy. The word declares that those that seek to follow a Holy God must be holy.

As you look back at your life, you will recognize that in your ignorance, your walk did not always please God. You sought to satisfy the lusts that influenced you. Now that you are seeking to follow God, a change must be evident. Commit yourself to a holy conversation for God is an Holy God.

Day 18

Joshua 1:11 Pass through the host, and command the people, saying, Prepare you victuals; for within three days ye shall pass over this Jordan, to go in to possess the land, which the LORD your God giveth you to possess it.

Thought: You Have Been Prepared To Receive from the Lord the supplies that you need

Focus: It Is Time To Possess

God's conversation with Joshua first reminded the successor to Moses that the Lord was with him. He then directed Joshua to prepare the people to enter the land. They were to receive what God had promised them. It was their time to possess.

The various experiences God has brought you through have prepared you to receive what He has for you to receive. Your knowledge of His power, and your increased faith, has you where you need to be. It is your time to possess.

Day 19

Acts 1:8 But ye shall receive power, after that the Holy Ghost is come upon you: and ye shall be witnesses unto me both in Jerusalem, and in all Judaea, and in Samaria, and unto the uttermost part of the earth.

Thought: You Have Been Empowered to Tell The Story

Focus: The Story Must Be Told Everywhere

As Jesus prepared his disciples for their assignment, he instructed them of the need for the gospel to be shared everywhere. They would be empowered once they received the Holy Ghost, enabling them to accomplish the task. The story must be told.

God has poured His spirit into you, not only for you, but to share the story with others. The gospel message must be told to everyone. This includes your neighborhood, your relatives, and your co-workers. You have been empowered to tell the story.

Day 20

1 Peter 4:10 As every man hath received the gift, even so minister the same one to another, as good stewards of the manifold grace of God.

Thought: God Has Equipped You With A Gift

Focus: You Are Expected To Minister To Others

Peter reminds his readers that God has equipped each of them with a gift intended to be used to minister one to another. As good stewards, they must not allow their gift to remain dormant but continuously grow it. It was given to be used.

You have been given a gift, by God, that is to be used to be a blessing to others. As you commit yourself to developing your gift, stay focused on its purpose.

Day 21

Matthew 11:28-30 Come unto me, all ye that labour and are heavy laden, and I will give you rest. Take my yoke upon you, and learn of me; for I am meek and lowly in heart: and ye shall find rest unto your souls. For my yoke is easy, and my burden is light.

Thought: Your Burden Belongs In God's Hands

Focus: Rest Is Available

Jesus brought a message that was different from what the people were accustomed to. He made His invitation clear. There was no need for His followers to keep their burdens and be heavy laden. As they took the yoke of the Lord, they would learn of the Lord and find rest.

As you continue your journey with the Lord, it is essential that you understand that though you have responsibilities, your burdens belong in the hands of the Lord. Take the yoke, that Jesus offers, upon you. You will discover a God that can do more than you imagined and you will find rest that you did not realize was available.

Day 22

Nehemiah 4:6 So built we the wall; and all the wall was joined together unto the half thereof: for the people had a mind to work.

Thought: With The Proper Spirit Much Can Be Accomplished

Focus: One Is Not Enough; Success Demands All

Nehemiah was burdened with the condition of Jerusalem, he knew something had to be done. The walls must be built, the city must be repaired. He understood that the work demanded more than one or two individuals; it demanded the cooperation of all. With prayer and passion, he cast the vision to the people. With a mind to work, they received it and the wall was built.

How is the work of the Lord fulfilled? It must not be left to one or two, it requires a team, a team with a spirit to work. Commit yourself as a team player, joining with others who possess a positive spirit. As you labor together, the result will be great, much will be accomplished.

Day 23

Proverbs 16:7 When a man's ways please the LORD, he maketh even his enemies to be at peace with him.

Thought: Place Your Focus On God; Not On Your Enemies

Focus: Your Enemy Is Subject To God's Control

Focus is key in the life of a believer. It is a mistake to allow an enemy to cause one to make adjustments in their behavior. When one stays focused on pleasing God, they will discover that even their enemies will be at peace with them. All are subject to God's control.

As you endeavor to follow the Lord, there will be enemies that seek to distract you. Do not make the mistake, and make adjustments that compromise your walk with God, in order to please them. Stay focused on pleasing God. Your enemy is under God's control. He will cause them to be at peace with you.

Day 24

Romans 12:1 I beseech you therefore, brethren, by the mercies of God, that ye present your bodies a living sacrifice, holy, acceptable unto God, which is your reasonable service.

Thought: He Desires Not Just A Part, But All

Focus: It Is Our Reasonable Service

Paul, in the prior chapter, speaks of God's mercy and long suffering. His Word is not limited to any one group or just to those with a strong past, but to all. Realizing how loving God is, Paul beseeches his readers to present themselves totally to the Lord. He declares that it is their reasonable service.

What does God ask from those that seek to follow Him? Paul declares that we should present all of us as a living sacrifice. Understanding the fullness of God's love and concern for you, does He not deserve a total sacrifice? Is it not your reasonable service?

Day 25

Ephesians 3:20 Now unto him that is able to do exceeding abundantly above all that we ask or think, according to the power that worketh in us.

Thought: Stay Focused On The One That Is Able

Focus: God Has No Limits

Paul's words of encouragement seek to broaden our expectations of what is possible. As we stay focused on God, not quenching the power He has placed within us, more than we thought is possible. God has no limits.

There remains within us the struggle between our human intellect and what God is telling us. Our thoughts seek to limit God, while the Spirit is telling us what is possible. Stay focused on God, don't quench the power that is in you, and you will witness God moving beyond your imagination. He has no limits.

Day 26

John 13:14-15 If I then, your Lord and Master, have washed your feet; ye also ought to wash one another's feet. For I have given you an example, that ye should do as I have done to you.

Thought: Seek To Serve Not To Be Served

Focus: The Example Is Clear

Living in today's society provides a paradigm that is contrary to the ways of the Lord. As you seek to be used by the Lord, it is essential that you keep a servant's spirit and heart.

Your focus must be on serving, not on being served. Your greatness will be displayed in how well you serve others.

Day 27

Colossians 4:5-6 Walk in wisdom toward them that are without, redeeming the time. Let your speech be alway with grace, seasoned with salt, that ye may know how ye ought to answer every man.

Thought: With Wisdom and Grace Share with Others

Focus: Your Response Matters

Each child of God has the opportunity to bless those that know not the Lord. When these opportunities arise it is essential that wisdom and grace is used. Godly wisdom is an essential quality for those that desire to bless others.

As you interact with those outside the body of Christ, wisdom is essential if you are going to add value to their lives. Your words should be spoken with grace, seasoned with salt, that your responses will have the intended impact.

Day 28

Acts 6:8 And Stephen, full of faith and power, did great wonders and miracles among the people.

Thought: You Have Been Empowered To Accomplish

Focus: Your Assignment Is Not Simply To Have A Title: You Have Been Empowered To Make A Difference

As the growing church required others to serve, Stephen was among the seven appointed as a Deacon. The scripture tells us he did more than have a title. Wonders and miracles were accomplished throughout his life. He was empowered to accomplish.

A title or office without works means little to God. Those that have assignments are expected, through their commitment and anointing, to accomplish much. There is no need for anyone to have a title if nothing is being done. You have been empowered to make a difference.

Day 29

Numbers 23:19 God is not a man, that he should lie; neither the son of man, that he should repent: hath he said, and shall he not do it? or hath he spoken, and shall he not make it good?

Thought: Man May Lie; God Cannot

Focus: What He Has Spoken Will Come To Pass

Balak, king of the Moabites, offered a great reward to the prophet Balaam if he would curse the people of God. Balaam was willing to do so but God would not allow it to take place. Balaam had to explain to the King that what God has blessed no man can curse. God had chosen to bless Israel and His word would be fulfilled. God is unable to lie nor is He able to repent. What He has spoken will come to pass.

You will learn, as you walk with God, that His Word is the final answer. Regardless of what man might want to change, they have not the power or authority to do so. Whom God blesses man cannot curse. God has chosen you to be a recipient of His blessings and as long as you continue to walk in His will, no one can change that. God's promises will be fulfilled, He can not lie nor will He repent.

Day 30

Joshua 1:8 This book of the law shall not depart out of thy mouth; but thou shalt meditate therein day and night, that thou mayest observe to do according to all that is written therein: for then thou shalt make thy way prosperous, and then thou shalt have good success.

Thought: Success Is Found In The Word of God

Focus: Stay Focused; Stay Blessed

Leadership is complex. Leaders are approached for guidance and counsel, as well as being challenged on decisions they make. Their responses are critical, as others make their decisions based on what is shared. Knowing this, the Lord told Joshua to place his total focus on the Word of God, meditating upon it day and night. All that would come out of his mouth was to be Word based. Success would follow.

The key to true success is found in the Word of God. As you commit yourself to the Word, to both observe and share, the truth it provides will cause success to follow. Your thoughts and logic must be shaped through the Word. It will allow you to bless others and to bless yourself.

Day 31

Joshua 14:12 Now therefore give me this mountain, whereof the LORD spake in that day; for thou heardest in that day how the Anakims were there, and that the cities were great and fenced: if so be the LORD will be with me, then I shall be able to drive them out, as the LORD said.

Thought: What Is Yours Is Yours

Focus: When God Made The Promise He Knew What Would Occur

Forty-five years earlier, God committed the mountain Caleb saw to be his. It appeared to Joshua that his friend was now perhaps too old to fight those that possessed the mountain. He suggested that Caleb accept another piece of land that he would not have to fight for. Caleb rejected that thought, declaring that God had kept him strong throughout the years. When God made the promise He knew how many years would pass. His promise would be fulfilled.

Waiting on God can be challenging, especially when weeks become months and the months become years. The key is remaining focused on the promise and not allowing any delays to cloud the fact God made the promise. Remind yourself that God knew all that would occur when He made His promise. Others might think it is too late but His promise will be fulfilled.

Day 32

2 Chronicles 7:15 Now mine eyes shall be open, and mine ears attent unto the prayer that is made in this place.

Thought: The Right Spirit Gains God's Attention

Focus: Your Prayer Will Be Heard

After the building of the Temple was completed, Solomon appealed to the Lord that it would be a place, where in the midst of a storm, the people could come and seek the face of God. The Lord responded by declaring that, if they came with humility and a repented heart, He would respond to their cries. His eyes would be open and His ears attentive to their prayer. The right spirit would gain God's attention.

As you find yourself in the midst of a great storm, you as a child of God, have the privilege of going before your God. As you go forth with a repentant heart and a spirit of humility, you have the assurance of knowing He will be attentive to your cry. His eyes will be open and His ears listening to your prayers. Your right spirit will bring a response.

Day 33

Mathew 14:27-29 But straightway Jesus spake unto them, saying, Be of good cheer; it is I; be not afraid. And Peter answered him and said, Lord, if it be thou, bid me come unto thee on the water. And he said, Come. And when Peter was come down out of the ship, he walked on the water, to go to Jesus.

Thought: In Every Storm There Is A Lesson

Focus: You Are Coming Out Stronger Than When You Went In

Every storm is not the same, but in each one there is a lesson to learn. Peter, along with all of the Apostles, found themselves in a God created storm. While the others panicked, Peter saw it as a lesson to extend his faith. Confirming that it was Jesus, he requested that the Master would bid him to come. He believed, as he saw Jesus' walking, he also could walk on the water. He saw the storm as a growth opportunity. There was a lesson to be learned.

As you face the Coronavirus storm there is a lesson to be learned. Yours may not be the same as another, but it is needed in your life. Avoid any panic, but prayerfully ask the Lord to reveal the lesson(s) to be learned in your life. Don't hesitate to ask Him to bid you to come. As He directs, obey. You are coming out stronger than when you went in.

Day 34

Proverbs 3:6 In all thy ways acknowledge him, and he shall direct thy paths.

Thought: Before Taking Action Seek The Lord

Focus: True Faith Is Demonstrated By Obedience To His Directions

The Proverb directs us to place our total trust in the Lord. We are, before taking any action, to acknowledge Him. He will lead us in the proper direction. His knowledge is not limited to yesterday but also includes tomorrow. Those that seek Him have the joy of knowing they will be led right.

As you face the challenges of the Coronavirus you need not be uncertain as to what action to take. As you place your trust in the Lord, you can, with confidence, be assured of making the best decisions. As you are following the Lord's directions you are displaying your faith. Before acting seek the Lord.

Day 35

Psalm 32:8-9 I will instruct thee and teach thee in the way which thou shalt go: I will guide thee with mine eye. Be ye not as the horse, or as the mule, which have no understanding: whose mouth must be held in with bit and bridle, lest they come near unto thee.

Thought: As God Instructs, Obey

Focus: His Instructions, When Followed, Will End In Joy

Within this psalm, David speaks to the need of acknowledging his transgressions and of the Lord being his hiding place. He also speaks of the importance of obeying the instructions of the Lord. As God provides direction it is essential that obedience follows. We must not be as the mule which has no understanding. His instructions are to be followed.

As you recognize and accept that God has knowledge of not just today, but also of tomorrow, it should help you to be obedient to His directions. As He leads you into places of safety and victory, obey freely. It is through your obedience that you will discover great joy.

Day 36

Genesis 26:24 And the Lord appeared unto him the same night, and said, I am the God of Abraham thy father: fear not, for I am with thee, and bless thee, and multiply thy seed for my servant Abraham's sake.

Thought: Fear Not; Before You Were Born, God Chose To Bless You

Focus: You Are A Part Of God's Plan To Bless Others

While in the midst of a struggle with the herdsmen of Gerar, over the ownership of a series of wells, the Lord spoke to Issac. He assured Isaac there was no need for him to fear. The Lord had chosen, for Abraham's sake, to bless him. He was to be a blessing to others.

It is difficult, at times, to understand why God blesses whom He does. It becomes clearer when you recognize that His plan does not begin with the birth of the individual. Before you were born, God chose you to be a blessing to others. In the midst of any struggles you may face, you need not fear for the Lord is with you.

Day 37

Deuteronomy 8:2 And thou shalt remember all the way which the Lord thy God led thee these forty years in the wilderness, to humble thee, and to prove thee, to know what was in thine heart, whether thou wouldest keep his commandments, or no.

Thought: There Is A Purpose To Your Journey

Focus: You Are Being Prepared For The Journey That Is Before You.

As Israel came to the end of their wilderness journey, Moses reminded them to give thought to what had occurred. They had spent forty years being shown that God was their provider. Through this period, they were being taught the necessity of obedience. God humbled them to prove what was in their hearts. They were being prepared to receive the promise that awaited them. There was a purpose for their journey.

There is a purpose to every part of your journey. The parts that you tend to shy away from may be the most important. Yes, God will take you through periods where you have no other choice but to depend upon Him. As He humbles you, maintain a spirit of obedience. You are being prepared for the blessings that are before you.

Day 38

Luke 2:20 And the shepherds returned, glorifying and praising God for all the things that they had heard and seen, as it was told unto them.

Thought: You Have Seen Too Much Not To Praise Him

Focus: Your Life Has Been Changed Forever

A group of shepherds were in the field tending to their flocks. While they were there, God sent an angel to share the message of the birth of the Christ child with them. What they were experiencing would change their lives forever. They had heard the praising of the heavenly host and were now about to see the Christ child. After witnessing the babe in the manger, they left glorying and praising God. Their lives had been changed forever.

God reveals Himself to His children. You have witnessed various incidents that have provided you sufficient evidence of God's glory. As the shepherds, you have seen too much not to praise Him. Rejoice in knowing that your life has been changed forever.

Day 39

Luke 2:26 And it was revealed unto him by the Holy Ghost, that he should not see death, before he had seen the Lord's Christ.

Thought: Be Sensitive to The Spirit; He Has Much To Reveal

Focus: The Spirit Speaks Today What Will Occur Tomorrow

Simeon was a faithful child of God, one that understood the prophecies found in the scriptures. He also was sensitive to the voice of the Spirit. It was the Spirit that revealed to Simeon that, before he died, he would see the Christ child. The Spirit was accurate, it occurred just as He said.

God speaks both through His Word and His Spirit. Both provide accurate information. As the Spirit speaks to you it is essential that you hearken to His voice. He can declare today what will occur tomorrow. Your blessings become available through your obedience. Obey and be blessed.

Day 40

Hebrews 11:6 But without faith it is impossible to please him: for he that cometh to God must believe that he is, and that he is a rewarder of them that diligently seek him.

Thought: Pleasing God Requires Faith

Focus: Rewards Come To Those That Seek Him

Pleasing God is the goal of every child of God. Accomplishing this requires faith. Faith that demonstrates both trust and obedience in God. Faith responds to both the Word and the Spirit. Faith seeks the Lord for needs to be met and His will to be accomplished.

As you walk with the Lord, occasions will arise where faith will be required. As you respond to the Lord's direction you will be positioning yourself to receive. In addition to receiving, you will be pleasing God. It is your faith that He honors. As, by faith, you seek Him you shall be rewarded.

Day 41

Acts 3:12 And when Peter saw it, he answered unto the people, Ye men of Israel, why marvel ye at this? or why look ye so earnestly on us, as though by our own power or holiness we had made this man to walk?

Thought: Never Forget Where Your Power Comes From

Focus: Without God You Are Powerless

After watching one, who had for years been begging for alms, up praising God the people marveled. Their attention was on Peter and John, believing that somehow they were the one's that healed this lame man. Peter quickly responded. This is not a man thing, this is a God thing, the power came from Jesus, the one you crucified. He understood where his power came from.

It is God's will to work through you to bless lives. Through your walk with Him, signs and wonders are to occur. It is essential, that as they do, you continuously remind yourself and others what the source of your power is. Never forget that without God you have no power.

Day 42

Genesis 12:4 So Abram departed, as the Lord had spoken unto him; and Lot went with him: and Abram was seventy and five years old when he departed out of Haran.

Thought: The Journey Has Just Begun

Focus: Your Obedience Is Essential

At the transition of Abram's father, the Lord spoke to his servant, reminding him of the directions he was given while yet in Ur. He was to leave his home and kindred and journey to the land God had for him. Abram responded by departing. Throughout the journey Abram would learn the importance of obedience. It was through obedience that the fullness of God's blessings would flow into his life.

Your walk with God is intended to bring you to a place determined by Him. As He directs your steps, you will learn that your complete obedience is essential. As you walk with God, there will be times you will be uncertain of how your way will be made. It is at those times when your obedience is key. Be assured, as you go forward, you are being led to a place of complete victory.

Day 43

Joshua 3:13 And it shall come to pass, as soon as the soles of the feet of the priests that bear the ark of the Lord, the Lord of all the earth, shall rest in the waters of Jordan, that the waters of Jordan shall be cut off from the waters that come down from above; and they shall stand upon an heap.

Thought: Your Faith Must Be Tested

Focus: Your Victory Will Follow Your Test

The experiences we face allow for our faith to grow. Israel, when they approached the Red Sea, displayed their lack of faith. They accused God of bringing them into the wilderness to die. The Lord, despite their doubts, opened the waters allowing them to go forth on dry land. The crossing of the Jordan River was different. Led by the priests, the waters remained intact until they stepped into the water. Their faith had to be tested; victory followed

There will be tests that arise that will produce an opportunity for you to demonstrate your faith. Each test will bring you to a higher level. As the Lord leads you, do not allow fear to deter you. Beyond your test victory will follow.

Day 44

Proverbs 15:29 The Lord is far from the wicked: but he heareth the prayer of the righteous.

Thought: Your Godly Lifestyle Has God's Attention

Focus: Your Prayers Will Be Heard

Prayer is a greater weapon than most recognize. When coupled with a Godly lifestyle, it has the ability to totally change situations. Don't see prayer as simply an obligation but rather as a weapon that has God's attention. His ears await your cries.

Unfortunately, prayer is often not understood. It is the vehicle that the Lord has given us to enter into His presence. It provides us the opportunity to both hear His voice and to make our requests known unto Him. As one that lives Godly be assured that your prayers will be heard.

Day 45

Luke 6:27-28 But I say unto you which hear, Love your enemies, do good to them which hate you, Bless them that curse you, and pray for them which despitefully use you.

Thought: Godly Love Is Extended To All

Focus: Your Enemies Are Included In Whom To Love

It is common to observe individuals that share love with those that love them back. It is much less common for love to be demonstrated towards those that might be described as enemies. Though it may be difficult, it is both necessary and possible. It is through God's love that one is able to go beyond the norm. Godly love is extended to all.

Yesterday was Valentine's Day, a time that love is extended to those that are close to one another. Husbands and wives, boyfriends and girlfriends share their appreciation and fondness for one another. Godly love goes beyond those limits. With Godly love, prayers and concern is shared with all, including one's enemies.

Day 46

Psalm 27:1 The Lord is my light and my salvation; whom shall I fear? the Lord is the strength of my life; of whom shall I be afraid?

Thought: Fear Has No Place In The Life Of A Saint

Re: Your Strength Comes From The Lord

David, whose lineage traces back to Hagar, a Hamite woman, faced a variety of enemies. His testimony was plain. There was no place for fear in his life, he did not need to be afraid of any of his enemies. David's strength came from the Lord. He was confident of victory.

When dependency against one's enemies is solely upon personal strength, it is easy to understand how fear enters in. The child of God is not limited to their own resources; the Lord is their strength. With confidence, you can face any enemy. The Lord is your salvation; you need not be afraid of anyone.

Day 47

Genesis 41:45 And Pharaoh called Joseph's name Zaphnath-paneah; and he gave him to wife Asenath the daughter of Potipherah priest of On. And Joseph went out over all the land of Egypt.

Thought: Joseph's Sons, Manasseh And Ephraim Were Hamites

Focus: Joshua Was A Descendent Of Ham

As we trace the lineage of Joshua, we discover Joseph and his Egyptian wife, the daughter of an Egyptian priest. Noting that Egypt was developed by Mizraim, the son of Ham, we are able to establish that Joshua, himself, was a descendent of Ham.

A study of the scriptures reveals countless examples of men and women that, though is it not generally known, are decedents of Ham. It is through scripture that we discover an accurate account of Ham's role in history. It is an account that has been lost to most. It is an account that must be discovered. Throughout this month we will endeavor to uncover many of these men and women.

Day 48

Mathew 5:13 Ye are the salt of the earth: but if the salt have lost his savour, wherewith shall it be salted? it is thenceforth good for nothing, but to be cast out, and to be trodden under foot of men.

Thought: Stay In The Race; Your Influence Matters

Focus: To Remain You Must Follow His Pattern

Jesus reminded His followers of their importance to others; they are the salt of the world. Their lives are to demonstrate, to all, the importance and joy of following the Lord. They were also reminded if their lives do not reflect the Lord's they would be discarded from the race. To remain they must follow His pattern.

As a child of God, one that lives a Godly life, you have the privilege of influencing others. You are the salt of the world. It is essential that you not only start the race but continue in a Godly manner. If your life no longer reflects Godliness you will be eliminated from the race. Stay in the race; your influence matters.

Day 49

Matthew 5:6 Blessed are they which do hunger and thirst after righteousness: for they shall be filled.

Thought: The Proper Appetite Is Required To Be Filled

Focus: Am I Hungry Enough?

With the disciples sitting at the feet of Jesus, he shared with them key points of his teachings. In this verse, Jesus declares that those that hunger and thirst for righteousness shall be filled. It brings to mind two questions. First, how large is my appetite and second, what am I hungry for? Wholeness comes to those that have the proper diet and are not satisfied with just a portion of the meal.

What are you hungry for, what drives you? Your appetite will determine your behavior. If you are seeking to use God to obtain what you want in life, apart from His will, you will be left empty. As you commit yourself to pleasing the Lord and give yourself to growth, the end will leave you full. "He that hungers and thirst after righteousness shall be filled."

Day 50

Acts 3:6 Then Peter said, Silver and gold have I none; but such as I have give I thee: In the name of Jesus Christ of Nazareth rise up and walk.

Thought: If You Pray, You Have The Power To Change Lives

Focus: Prayer Is What Connects You With God

There are many essential elements needed for a successful relationship with the Lord. We must be students of the Word, we must be both praisers and worshippers, but the key is our prayer life. It is our connection to Him and what brings change. Praying people have the power to change lives.

Peter was a praying person, he with John on his side, were on their way to the Temple to pray. Being led by the Spirit, Peter spoke change into the lame man's life. You and I, if we are praying people, have the same power. Connect with the Lord and have the authority to change lives.

Day 51

Acts 2:42-43 And they continued stedfastly in the apostles' doctrine and fellowship, and in breaking of bread, and in prayers. And fear came upon every soul: and many wonders and signs were done by the apostles.

Thought: The Victory Begins With The "They"

Focus: The Church Is A Body; The Parts Are Interdependent

When we look at the success of the early church we must note what made the difference. The verse begins with a key phrase, "they prayed". Though the signs and wonders came through the Apostles, it was the prayers of each member that laid the foundation for the success. The church is a body with all the parts being interdependent in each other.

Both leaders and followers need to understand the need for each other. Leaders must lead but the strength of the congregation comes through the prayers of all. Success begins with the "they". The signs will follow.

Day 52

1 Peter 5:8-9 Be sober, be vigilant; because your adversary the devil, as a roaring lion, walketh about, seeking whom he may devour: Whom resist stedfast in the faith, knowing that the same afflictions are accomplished in your brethren that are in the world.

Thought: You Will Come Under Attack; Your Victory Is In The Word

Focus: You Are Equipped To Win

Peter shares, in these verses, the recipe of victory when the enemy attacks. It is essential that the child of God remains sober minded as well as watchful; recognizing that both those in the church and those in the world will face satanic assaults. The difference is in the response. As the child of God remains committed to the Word and walks in faith they will come forth victorious.

The fact that you walk with God does not mean that you will not face the attacks of the enemy. It is your faith that will provide you victory. With a commitment to the Word, resist the enemy's desire to sift you. Others may fall but you will be victorious.

Day 53

Luke 1:18 And Zacharias said unto the angel, Whereby shall I know this? for I am an old man, and my wife well stricken in years.

Thought: Yes, The Impossible Is Possible

Focus: God Has No Limits

It was not simply the passing of time from when he prayed for a son that caused Zacharias to question what he heard. He knew that both he and his wife Elizabeth were no longer able to bear children. It was impossible. What he did not consider was that with God all things are possible, even the impossible.

The human mind decides what is possible and what is not. Jesus did not disagree with that determination, but what he did declare was that what was impossible for man was possible for God. The Lord has no limits. As He directs your faith to go forward, obey. With God, all things are possible, even the impossible.

Day 54

1 Peter 2:9 But ye are a chosen generation, a royal priesthood, an holy nation, a peculiar people; that ye should shew forth the praises of him who hath called you out of darkness into his marvellous light.

Thought: God Called Us To Demonstrate His Goodness

Focus: Some Praises Are Spoken, Others Are Lived

As children of the Lord we must understand our calling. We are to live that others might see the Lord through us. It is proper that we speak of the goodness of the Lord, but our actions are able to declare, in a greater manner, who He is. We have been called to demonstrate His goodness.

God has called you to live a life that others might see the goodness of the Lord. Recognizing that your behavior speaks louder than your words, commit yourself to a Godly life. Enjoy the privilege of revealing who the Lord is to those who don't listen to words.

Day 55

Psalm 111:10 The fear of the Lord is the beginning of wisdom: a good understanding have all they that do his commandments: his praise endureth for ever.

Thought: Obedience Leads To Understanding

Focus: True Wisdom Begins With God

There is both earthly wisdom and Godly wisdom. Those that fear, or better said, reverence, the Lord received the latter. As they continue in His will, through obedience to His commandments, they gain understanding.

If your journey through life is to be successful, it must begin with the acknowledgement of God and a reverence for who He is. As you obey His commandments, you will be positioning yourself to gain insight to the ways of the Lord, resulting in a victorious walk.

Day 56

Proverbs 18:16 A man's gift maketh room for him, and bringeth him before great men.

Thought: Develop Your Gift; Don't Promote It

Focus: Your Gift Is Given From God

Unfortunately, in the church world, we witness many who instead of simply developing the gift God has given them, they seek to promote it. It is their desire to be in a position of power and status. This is unfortunate. God gifts His children as He sees fit, and is the One that chooses when and how they are to be used.

You have been blessed by the Lord to add value to His Kingdom. You have a responsibility to develop your gift, not to promote it. By God's timing, your gift will make room for you and will be put into full use. Remain patient, knowing your gift has been given for God's purpose not yours.

Day 57

Romans 12:14 Bless them which persecute you: bless, and curse not.

Thought: Good Has the Power To Overcome Evil

Focus: Respond With Good When Evil Occurs

We live during a time where evil continues to show itself. This past weekend, eleven individuals lost their lives simply because of their religious belief. Repeatedly, others have been killed because of the color of their skin. How does one respond to these acts of evil? God's Word speaks clearly, good has the power to overcome evil. As we mourn the lives of those of whose lives were taken, we must also mourn the current spirit of our country. As we mourn, we cannot allow the evil of others to cause us to respond in kind. God's Word remains true, good has the power to overcome evil.

In our individual lives we also face evil. There are some that will seek to curse you. Regardless of what your emotions may say, God's Word must control your behavior. As the Lord has directed, bless those that curse you, overcome evil with good. Good does have the power to overcome evil.

Day 58

Acts 4:31 And when they had prayed, the place was shaken where they were assembled together; and they were all filled with the Holy Ghost, and they spake the word of God with boldness.

Thought: Prayer Brings Results

Focus: Your Cries Will Not Go Unnoticed

When the Apostles came against strong opposition they joined together and cried unto the Lord. Their petitions did not go unnoticed by the Lord. He responded by shaking where they were assembled and filled all with the Holy Spirit. Prayer brings results.

In the midst of your greatest challenges do not allow fear to overcome you. The answer to your situation is prayer. Let your prayers go forth before the Lord; He will respond.

Day 59

John 8:31-32 Then said Jesus to those Jews which believed on him, If ye continue in my word, then are ye my disciples indeed; And ye shall know the truth, and the truth shall make you free.

Thought: Pursue Truth; It Has The Power To Set You Free

Focus: Your Search Will Take You To God's Word

Jesus spent much time sharing truth. Many rejected it, choosing to attack him. Others took a different approach, believing what they heard. To them Jesus gave instruction. They must continue in his Word, which when followed, would set them free.

We live in a time where truth is not honored. As a child of God, it is essential that you dwell in God's Word, with a commitment to obey. Through your commitment to truth, you will discover that it has the power to set you free.

Day 60

John 4:24 God is a Spirit: and they that worship him must worship him in spirit and in truth.

Thought: Worship Demands Both Commitment And Knowledge

Focus: True Worship Is The Only Worship Honored

During his conversation with the woman at the well, Jesus spoke of "true worship". There must be a complete commitment of one's spirit, as well as an accurate knowledge of God. Without spirit and truth there cannot be true worship.

As we observe the many who offer words of worship, you are aware true worship is not always present. As you present your words of worship, let it be with both a knowledge of a holy God and a total commitment of your spirit. Offer true worship, the only worship that is honored.

Day 61

Matthew 11:1 And it came to pass, when Jesus had made an end of commanding his twelve disciples, he departed thence to teach and to preach in their cities.

Thought: The Gospel Needs To Be Preached In Every City

Focus: Your City Is Included

The gospel message must be carried everywhere. Jesus demonstrated the importance to the Apostles of having the message shared by bringing it to their cities. At times, while bringing the message elsewhere, we forget about home. All cities, including our own, need to hear about Jesus.

In realizing the importance of the message of salvation, we must not neglect our own community. It is proper that you share with others but don't forget about your own community. Let all hear about Jesus.

Day 62

Romans 12:14 Bless them which persecute you: bless, and curse not.

Thought: When Under Attack Stay Godly; Bless The Attacker

Focus: Humility Is Essential

The typical response when one comes under attack is to retaliate. Though this is the common reaction, it is not what pleases God. The appropriate response is to bless and not to curse. This will not be accomplished without a spirit of humility abiding in the individual.

In the life of every saint, attacks will take place. As you are victimized, your spiritual growth will be tested. With a spirit of humility, endeavor to overcome evil with good. Bless them that curse you. Your behavior will both honor God and provide an opportunity for a soul to be won.

Day 63

Ephesians 4:16 From whom the whole body fitly joined together and compacted by that which every joint supplieth, according to the effectual working in the measure of every part, maketh increase of the body unto the edifying of itself in love.

Thought: Growth Comes From Cooperation And Participation

Focus: Your Role Is Critical

For growth to take place within any congregation certain factors are essential. There must be an understanding of the importance of each member's role and there must be cooperation. Each part has a specific and unique role to play; all of which are important. As each part functions properly growth will take place.

Do you realize how important your role within the Kingdom is? The Lord has equipped and placed you within the body to work in cooperation with others. As you do growth will occur. Members will grow and others will be added to the Church. Growth comes from cooperation and participation.

Day 64

Hebrews 13:5 Let your conversation be without covetousness; and be content with such things as ye have: for he hath said, I will never leave thee, nor forsake thee.

Thought: Be Assured The Lord Is Always Present

Focus: His Consistency Is Without Fail

As our time at Hilton Head Island comes to a close, I took a walk on the beach. As I enjoyed the Lord's creation, I noticed the consistency of the waves. Each day, at the prescribed time, the waves came onto the beach. It made me think of the consistency of the Lord. Regardless of the weather or season, the tides will be exactly where they are to be. There consistency is without fail.

As your journey continues, with the Lord, you will have a variety of circumstances. People and factors will alter, at times beyond your control. In spite of the ups and downs, be assured that the Lord is always present. At the prescribed time, He will accomplish all that needs to be done. He will not fail.

Day 65

Acts 16:25 And at midnight Paul and Silas prayed, and sang praises unto God: and the prisoners heard them.

Thought: Those That Pray Will Praise Him

Focus: Do Not Let Circumstances Take Your Praise

Paul and Silas were placed in prison after Paul cast out a demonic spirit from a young woman. The charges came from those that were profiting from her ability to tell the future. The men of God found themselves, after being beaten, in stocks in the inner prison. They responded with prayer and songs of praises that all could hear. The Lord honored their faith by sending an earthquake. The foundations of the prison were shook and all were set free. Their circumstances did not impact their praise.

In life, challenging times come to all, saints and sinners alike. As you develop a strong relationship, based on prayer, nothing will stop your praise. Let your life be an example to all. Regardless of what you face let your prayers go forth. Your praise and your deliverance will follow.

Day 66

Colossians 4:6 Let your speech be always with grace, seasoned with salt, that ye may know how ye ought to answer every man.

Thought: Your Words Matter; Give Thought Before You Speak

Focus: What Is The Intent Of Your Words

As one begins a conversation, thought must be given to what one is seeking to accomplish, what is the intent of the conversation. Prayerfully, with a desire to encourage, consideration is given to the words that will be used. The scripture reminds us to season our words with grace. Our words matter, they must be chosen carefully.

The Lord has blessed you to be able to encourage others as you share the Good News. To accomplish this, it is essential that careful thought is given to what words you use. Remembering your intent, season your words with grace; you will be a blessing to many.

Day 67

Joel 2:25 And I will restore to you the years that the locust hath eaten, the cankerworm, and the caterpiller, and the palmerworm, my great army which I sent among you.

Thought: What You Thought Was Lost Forever Shall Be Restored

Focus: God Has A Plan To Bless You

Israel, as a result of their failure to follow God, found themselves in the midst of suffering at His hands. As bleak as things looked, Joel shared a word of hope. The Lord committed Himself to restore to His people all that they had lost. What they thought was lost forever was now going to be restored.

In life, though mistakes, loss occurs. It is easy to understand how faith diminishes during these challenging times. If you find yourself in such a situation, do not give up hope. Stay prayerful, stay focused, stay positive, for the Lord is able to restore all that which has been lost. God has a plan to bless you.

Day 68

Psalm 120:1 In my distress I cried unto the Lord, and he heard me.

Thought: The Lord Awaits Your Cry

Focus: Don't Panic; Pray

David, as he faced the attacks of his enemies, refused to panic or concede defeat. He chose rather to pray. He was confident that as he would cry unto the Lord, his prayers would be heard. David was not disappointed, the Lord delivered him out of all of his fears.

You will face challenging times. How you respond is critical to your future. If you accept defeat, Satan will continue to push against you, if you panic, your reason for hope will vanish, your only solution is to pray. As you cry to the Lord He will respond to your petition. Deliverance is on its way.

Day 69

1 Timothy 4:14 Neglect not the gift that is in thee, which was given thee by prophecy, with the laying on of the hands of the presbytery.

Thought: The Gift Is There; It Must Be Used

Focus: You Are An Important Part Of The Puzzle

Recognizing what God had placed within Timothy, Paul reminded him of the importance of his gift. It was essential that his gift was not neglected, it was a vital part of the gospel being shared. He was an important part of the puzzle.

Regardless of what your gift might be, it is an important part of the gospel being received by others. Do not allow your gift to lie dormant. Give yourself to growth that God might be glorified, and others might know the blessings of salvation. You are an important part of the puzzle.

Day 70

Philippians 3:13-14 Brethren, I count not myself to have apprehended: but this one thing I do, forgetting those things which are behind, and reaching forth unto those things which are before, I press toward the mark for the prize of the high calling of God in Christ Jesus.

Thought: Leave Yesterday In The Past And Reach For Tomorrow

Focus: There Is A Mark That Awaits Your Press

Even though Paul's knowledge of God was extensive, he continued to press for more. He did not compare himself with others, but rather saw the perfection of Jesus. With his focus on the Lord, regardless of any opposition he faced, he continued. Yesterday was left behind and tomorrow was reached for.

You, as others, have achieved a place in God. During your journey, you made some sound decisions as well as with others failed to meet the mark. It is essential that you do not compromise with less than what God intends for your life. As you thank Him for what He has done, keep reaching. There is a mark before you.

Day 71

2 Kings 20:2 Then he turned his face to the wall, and prayed unto the Lord, saying,

Thought: In The Midst Of Your Greatest Challenges Don't Give Up, Pray

Focus: Prayer Can Accomplish the Impossible

Hezekiah had just received a message from the Lord shared by the prophet Elisha. He was told that he would not be healed; he was going to die. Elisha refused to accept the message as final; he chose to pray. The impossible was accomplished, his prayer was heard, fifteen years were added to his life.

In the midst of your greatest challenges you may be tempted to yield all hope of deliverance. Regardless of how dismal things may look you need not give up. As Hezekiah did, turn your face to the wall and pray. With God the impossible is possible.

Day 72

Luke 24:49 And, behold, I send the promise of my Father upon you: but tarry ye in the city of Jerusalem, until ye be endued with power from on high.

Thought: Let Your Waiting Be With Positive Expectation

Focus: God's Promises Will Be Fulfilled

The last conversation Jesus had with his disciples included his instructions for them to wait in Jerusalem, where they would be endued with "power from on high". In not many days they would receive the promise of the Father. They waited, with great expectation, and were not disappointed. The promise was fulfilled.

As the Lord speaks to you through His Word, and His Spirit, you have the assurance that everyone of His promises will be fulfilled. With joy, and expectation, wait as God brings to pass all that He has promised. You will not be disappointed.

Day 73

2 Corinthians 9:6-7 But this I say, He which soweth sparingly shall reap also sparingly; and he which soweth bountifully shall reap also bountifully. Every man according as he purposeth in his heart, so let him give; not grudgingly, or of necessity: for God loveth a cheerful giver.

Thought: Give To Give; Not To Receive

Focus: God Honors The Cheerful Giver

As Paul encourages the saints to be liberal in their giving, he shares the principle of reaping and sowing. Those that sow bountifully will reap bountifully. God honors those that cheerfully give; those that give to give not to receive.

Giving is a spirit, one that all of us should seek to possess. A fellow minister shared an excellent concept with me. He declared, "I give because I have, I have because I give, therefore I am never without". Give to give not to receive; you will not be without.

Day 74

Luke 12:31 But rather seek ye the kingdom of God; and all these things shall be added unto you.

Thought: Seek God; The Rest Will Be Added

Focus: God Knows Exactly

The focus of those outside the church typically are the natural things of this world. The Lord instructed His followers in contrast, to seek the Kingdom of God. As they did, He would add the natural things to them. They needed not to worry for He knew exactly what they needed.

As you keep your attention on the things of the Lord, you will discover that you will not be left wanting. The Lord knows exactly what your needs are, and as you seek Him and the Kingdom, He has promised to meet each of them.

Day 75

1 Corinthians 2:4 And my speech and my preaching was not with enticing words of man's wisdom, but in demonstration of the Spirit and of power:

Thought: Your Power Is Derived Through The Spirit Not Your Wisdom

Focus: Stay Close Enough To God That He Might Work Through You

Paul was an extremely well educated man. Though he had a rich academic background, his trust was in the Spirit of the Lord. This is where his power was derived from. Paul knew where to put his trust, his faith was in the hands of the Lord.

Education is a good thing; being well versed in the Word of God adds value to one's life. It is well that you seek to learn, but never lose track of the fact that your power comes from the Spirit of the Lord.

Day 76

1 Peter 5:3 Neither as being lords over God's heritage, but being examples to the flock.

Thought: Those That Lead Must Set A Godly Example

Focus: Those You Lead Are God's Children Not Yours

As Peter gave direction to those that served as Elders, he emphasized their need to set an example. It was essential that they understood that those they led were God's children, not theirs. It is the leader's role to serve, not be served.

Not only leaders, but all of the people of God are to set an example for others. It must also be with a recognition that all God's children are just that, God's children. With a humble spirit, seek to bless those that God places into your life. The Lord in return will bless you.

Day 77

Acts 2:1-2 And when the day of Pentecost was fully come, they were all with one accord in one place. And suddenly there came a sound from heaven as of a rushing mighty wind, and it filled all the house where they were sitting.

Thought: As You Wait, Anticipate The Fulfillment Of The Lord's Promise

Focus: God's Spirit Flows Freely In The Midst Of Unity

The followers of Jesus, after his ascension, were sent to Jerusalem to wait to receive the promise of the Father. They were to receive the baptism of the Holy Spirit. With anticipation, and with one accord, they waited. They did not wait in vain, for at the time of God's choosing, they received the promise. In the midst of unity God's Spirit flowed freely.

It is the Lord's desire to utilize the local congregation. It is through a spirit of anticipation, and unity, that the Spirit of the Lord freely moves. As a part of the larger group, add value to the whole through a prayerful, and dedicated life to things of God. As you join with others, if like mind, you will experience the fullness of God's promises being fulfilled.

Day 78

Luke 22:31-32 And the Lord said, Simon, Simon, behold, Satan hath desired to have you, that he may sift you as wheat: But I have prayed for thee, that thy faith fail not: and when thou art converted, strengthen thy brethren.

Thought: At Your Weakest Moments The Prayers Of Jesus Will Sustain You

Focus: As He Strengthens You, Strengthen Others

Peter did not realize the extent of what he was going to face. In the midst of what he was to face his faith would falter. Jesus assured his disciple that though Satan sought to sift him, he had prayed for him. The Lord only requested that once Peter was strengthened, he would encourage his brethren.

In your journey you will face challenging times, some that will impact your faith. Be assured that prayers have been prayed for you. As you regain your strength and focus, through your experience, strengthen your brethren.

Day 79

Daniel 6:22 My God hath sent his angel, and hath shut the lions' mouths, that they have not hurt me: forasmuch as before him innocency was found in me; and also before thee, O king, have I done no hurt.

Thought: Remain Calm; Your Prayer Will Be Answered

Focus: Walk In His Will And Stay Confident

Daniel had a decision to make; He was told he could not pray to his God. With confidence, he continued to stay before God in prayer. He trusted that as he remained in the will of the Lord, God will intercede. He was not disappointed, God sent an angel to keep him safe.

The scriptures tell us to pray with thanksgiving. Regardless of any attack that comes against you, know that the Lord will respond to your petition. Knowing the Lord is with you, there is no need to allow fear to set in. As you remain in His will you have the right to expect victory. The Lord will not disappoint you.

Day 80

John 4:28-29 The woman then left her waterpot, and went her way into the city, and saith to the men, Come, see a man, which told me all things that ever I did: is not this the Christ?

Thought: Don't Allow Your Past To Keep You From Your Future

Focus: You Are Being Equipped To Bless Multitudes

After receiving and accepting what Jesus shared, the woman at the well left her water pot to go tell others of the good news. She was leaving her past that she might move into her future, a future that would bless many.

You are being prepared to bless others. As the Lord pours into your life, you will be required to let go of anything that might hinder your effectiveness. With joy, appreciate what God is doing in your life. Do not allow your past to keep you from your future.

Day 81

John 4:3-5 He left Judaea, and departed again into Galilee. And he must needs go through Samaria. Then cometh he to a city of Samaria, which is called Sychar, near to the parcel of ground that Jacob gave to his son Joseph.

Thought: Where There Is Someone Waiting, God Will Send His Word

Focus: When God Speaks, Listen And Receive

As Jesus left Judea carting the message of the gospel, he, by choice, entered Samaria. He was there to bring the Word to a single woman. She was hesitant at first to receive what Jesus was sharing, but once she did, she ran off to tell everyone about this man named Jesus. The Word was sent and she received it.

God is concerned about all of His creations. His message of salvation is intended for all. With a listening ear, be prepared to hear all that He has to say to you. Knowing your spirit, God will send His Word. Be ready to hear and obey. It is there to bless your life.

Day 82

2 Chronicles 7:14 If my people, which are called by my name, shall humble themselves, and pray, and seek my face, and turn from their wicked ways; then will I hear from heaven, and will forgive their sin, and will heal their land.

Thought: True Repentance Brings A Response

Focus: Repentance Has Required Action

Solomon sought God, asking that the newly built Temple would be a place that prayers of repentance could be offered. In response to Solomon's petition, the Lord committed Himself while providing a criteria. If the people would come humbly to pray, after turning from their ungodly behavior, and seek His face, He would hear and respond to their prayers. Forgiveness and healing would take place.

Within each of our journeys there will be mistakes made. The enemy will seek to use those times to separate you from God. Do not allow that to occur. Humble yourself and come before the Lord in prayer. With your prayer, cease from the behavior that grieved the Lord and seek His face. The Lord has committed Himself to respond. Forgiveness and healing will take place.

Day 83

Deuteronomy 30:19 I call heaven and earth to record this day against you, that I have set before you life and death, blessing and cursing: therefore choose life, that both thou and thy seed may live:

Thought: Both Blessings And Curses Are Before You

Focus: The Choice Is Yours, Choose Wisely

As Israel came to the end of their journey through the wilderness, about to enter the promised land, Moses directed them to the choice they had the power to make. God had made available to them the fullness of His blessings or the curses that would come through disobedience. It was their choice to make, the blessings or the curses.

As Israel had, each of us has the opportunity to choose what we receive from God. Our choice is demonstrated by our obedience or disobedience. Obedience to His Word brings His blessings while disobedience results in His curses. The choice is yours, choose wisely.

Day 84

Deuteronomy 28:1 And it shall come to pass, if thou shalt hearken diligently unto the voice of the Lord thy God, to observe and to do all his commandments which I command thee this day, that the Lord thy God will set thee on high above all nations of the earth:

Thought: You Have Been Prepared To Obey

Focus: It Is God's Will To Bless

For forty years Israel traveled through the wilderness. Their journey provided evidence of God's ability to bless. Manna was sent from heaven, water came from a rock, their clothes did not wear out, all declarations of God's power. As the journey was coming to an end, the Lord made His will known to the people; their obedience would be honored.

Your life is a journey. As the Lord takes you from place to place, He will demonstrate His ability to bless. As He provides for you, He expects your response to be one of obedience. In return for your obedience His blessings will flow into your life. You have been prepared to obey.

Day 85

Luke 24:49 And, behold, I send the promise of my Father upon you: but tarry ye in the city of Jerusalem, until ye be endued with power from on high.

Thought: The Promise Will Be Fulfilled

Focus: Wait With Confidence

The last directions Jesus gave his disciples was for them to wait in Jerusalem. It was there that they would receive the promise of the Father. Their waiting was to be done with confidence and with total focus on the Lord. There was no need to doubt; the promise would be fulfilled.

When the Lord makes a promise to you, one in which you must wait on, be careful to reject any thoughts of doubt. With confidence, stay focused on the Lord, for every word spoken by Him will come to pass. The promise will be fulfilled.

Day 86

Luke 24:45 Then opened he their understanding, that they might understand the scriptures,

Thought: Understanding Overcomes Doubt

Focus: Before You Tell Others, You Must First Believe Yourself

For forty days Jesus sought to bring his disciples to a place of faith. Even after, on a series of occasions, he showed himself to them it was not sufficient. Their joy and understanding only came when he opened their understanding to the scriptures. Then and only then were they ready to go forth with joy to share the gospel.

Your understanding of God's Word is essential to your ability to be an effective witness. Your actions and words must depict your belief in all that God has taught. Ask the Lord to open your understanding of God's Word. You will then be ready to go forth and tell others the good news.

Day 87

Psalm 71:4-5 Deliver me, O my God, out of the hand of the wicked, out of the hand of the unrighteous and cruel man. For thou art my hope, O Lord God: thou art my trust from my youth.

Thought: Don't Fight Your Way Out; Pray Your Way Out

Focus: God Is Your Deliverer

David faced many challenges in his life. As a man of faith, he quickly learned how to respond to them. Though he was a warrior, his deliverance did not come from his fighting. David, through prayer, put his trust in God; God was his deliverer.

When you come under attack it is essential that you know where to put your trust. With prayer, turn to the Lord. You can be assured that He will deliver you. Leave the fighting to others, your victory is coming from God.

Day 88

John 13:12-15. So after he had washed their feet, and had taken his garments, and was set down again, he said unto them, Know ye what I have done to you? Ye call me Master and Lord: and ye say well; for so I am. If I then, your Lord and Master, have washed your feet; ye also ought to wash one another's feet. For I have given you an example, that ye should do as I have done to you.

Thought: Christian Leaders Demonstrate Servanthood

Focus: Jesus Set The Example; We Are To Follow

It was essential to Jesus that His Disciples understood that leadership in the church must be different than leadership in the world. Mostly in the world, leaders are served, the opposite is to be true within the church. Jesus is the example, Christian leaders are servants to those that follow them.

As God blesses you to lead others, do not lose track of the example that Jesus gave as a leader. Accept your rightful role as a servant. Give of yourself, allowing God to use you to be a blessing to those that follow. Christian leaders demonstrate servanthood.

Day 89

John 21:17 He saith unto him the third time, Simon, son of Jonas, lovest thou me? Peter was grieved because he said unto him the third time, Lovest thou me? And he said unto him, Lord, thou knowest all things; thou knowest that I love thee. Jesus saith unto him, Feed my sheep.

Thought: Your Assignment Is Important To God

Focus: Serve With A Spirit Of Excellence

Shortly before the departure of Jesus, he questioned Peter about his love for the Lord. Each time Peter declared his love, he was instructed by Jesus, to feed his sheep. After the third time, Peter was grieved over the question. The questioning and directions came from the Lord, not to annoy but to demonstrate how important Peter's assignment was.

The assignment that God has placed under your control is key to the success of the ministry. Your love for the Lord will be demonstrated by your commitment to fulfilling your assignment, with a spirit of excellence. Your assignment is an important one.

Day 90

John 20:19 Then the same day at evening, being the first day of the week, when the doors were shut where the disciples were assembled for fear of the Jews, came Jesus and stood in the midst, and saith unto them, Peace be unto you.

Thought: Doubt Brings Forth Fear

Focus: Faith Must Take Charge

The disciples were slow to accept the fact that Jesus had risen from the dead. Their doubt resulted in fear, causing them to hide from the Jews. Jesus, realizing that their faith was essential, appeared before them bringing words of encouragement. Their faith took over, delivering them from their fear.

It is the desire of the Lord to utilize you for His will. For this you must walk in faith. Your enemy is the spirit of doubt. As the Lord reveals Himself to you step into faith. As faith takes charge joy will follow.

Day 91

Mark 1:35 And in the morning, rising up a great while before day, he went out, and departed into a solitary place, and there prayed.

Thought: Prayer Is Not An Event; It Is A Lifestyle

Focus: Does Your Day Start With Prayer?

Yesterday we celebrated the resurrection of Jesus. As we move forward in our lives, we would do well to consider what we have learned about the Lord. Consideration must be given not only to the power He possessed but to the source of His power; His prayer life. Prayer was not an event in His life but His lifestyle. It was common for Jesus to arise early and go to a solitary place and pray. Prayer was not an occasional event in His life, prayer was His lifestyle.

When do you pray? Is your prayer time limited to times of crisis or perhaps a formal structure? Though prayer at these times are important, it must not be the only times we pray. Make prayer a consistent part of your life, make it your lifestyle. Seek God for direction and insight. Through prayer, ask for wisdom as well as understanding. As you do, the Lord will provide all that you need. Start your day with prayer and remain in touch with the one that holds the blessings of tomorrow. Victory will follow.

Day 92

Luke 19:37 And when he was come nigh, even now at the descent of the mount of Olives, the whole multitude of the disciples began to rejoice and praise God with a loud voice for all the mighty works that they had seen.

Thought: His Acts Deserve A Praise

Focus: Have You Seen Enough?

As Jesus entered, on the colt, into Jerusalem, the multitude began to praise him. Though they did not fully understand who he was, they recognized that he came from God. It was the mighty acts they witnessed that caused them to offer their praises. It was a fact, they had seen enough to praise him. He deserved all of their praises.

In your walk with God, it is quite evident that God had showed Himself to you. His acts demonstrate both His love and His power. Surely you have witnessed enough to praise Him. He deserves all of your praises.

Day 93

Luke 21:19 In your patience possess ye your souls.

Thought: Stay Patient; God Will Lead You To Victory

Focus: In The Midst Of A Challenge Your Thoughts Must Be Kept In Check

In one of the last times Jesus spoke with His disciples, prior to His resurrection, He spoke of the many challenges they would face. Endeavoring to remind them of His promise to be with them, He spoke of the importance of their patience. They needed to remain patient, knowing He would direct them to victory.

Patience speaks to the confidence one has in Lord. It requires a knowledge and trust in the Word of God. As you face the challenges of life, it is essential that you keep your thoughts in check. As you stay patient, be assured that the Lord will bring you out victorious.

Day 94

Luke 22:42 Saying, Father, if thou be willing, remove this cup from me: nevertheless not my will, but thine, be done.

Thought: True Victory Is On The Other Side Of Submission

Focus: Yielding To His Will Is Essential

There are many types of prayer, but the one that may be called the most important is the prayer of submission. As Jesus went forth into the Garden of Gethsemane, he went to yield his flesh over to the will of God. Recognizing what laid before him, it was not easy, but he knew his yielding was essential.

No doubt your flesh is not pleased with all that you know is necessary. In your praying, let not your requests override your focus on submission. Learn to pray as Jesus did, not my will but your will be done. True victory is on the other side of submission.

Day 95

2 Corinthians 1:3-4 Blessed be God, even the Father of our Lord Jesus Christ, the Father of mercies, and the God of all comfort; Who comforteth us in all our tribulation, that we may be able to comfort them which are in any trouble, by the comfort wherewith we ourselves are comforted of God.

Thought: You Have Been Placed To Strengthen One In Need

Focus: As God Has Comforted You, Comfort Others

Each of us has faced times in which comfort has been difficult to find. It is at those times that the Lord extends His mercy unto us in our times of tribulation. As we receive His comfort, we are also learning the importance of reaching out to others with the same spirit. We have been equipped and prepared to strengthen those that have no strength.

After experiencing the comfort of God, you recognize the importance of reaching out to others. Not necessarily with words, but simply with your presence, you will be a blessing to those in need. You have been placed to strengthen someone in need.

Day 96

Hebrews 12:1 Wherefore seeing we also are compassed about with so great a cloud of witnesses, let us lay aside every weight, and the sin which doth so easily beset us, and let us run with patience the race that is set before us.

Thought: Hold Nothing Back; Release Everything

Focus: All Hinderances Must Be Let Go

The Bible provides us with a multitude of men and women who have walked by faith. Reminding us of this great cloud of witnesses, the author exhorts to follow their example in our walk with God. He shares the reality that if we are to accomplish this goal we must let go of the weights, and sin, we yet are carrying. All hindrances must be let go.

Is your walk with the Lord compromised by what you have not yet released? If so, you are missing the place God has for you. With a focused mind, let go of every weight and the sin, that will cause you to fall. As you release the hinderances from your life, you will soon experience the blessings, and joy, that only Jesus can provide. Hold nothing back, release all.

Day 97

Proverbs 4:23 Keep thy heart with all diligence; for out of it are the issues of life.

Thought: Good And Evil Begin In The Heart

Focus: How Well Are You Guarding Your Heart

Where does our behavior originate? Solomon warns us of the importance of "keeping" our heart for that is where the issues of life come from. It is essential that we understand that what we feed our heart shapes what comes from it. As one meditates continuously upon the Word of God that which flows will prove to be pleasing to the Lord.

What do you allow to enter your heart? If there are no controls placed upon what enters you will have little control over what leaves it. You must guard your heart from that which is not pleasing to the Lord. It is a reality that both good and evil begin in the heart.

Day 98

Luke 18:1 And he spake a parable unto them to this end, that men ought always to pray, and not to faint;

Thought: You Need Not Faint; You Can Pray

Focus: Your Victory Is On The Other Side Of Your Prayer

Throughout His earthly ministry, Jesus both taught and demonstrated the importance of prayer. One's prayer-life not only brings forth miracles but solidifies one's relationship with God. It is through prayer that we enter into the presence of God. It is through prayer that we are able to receive the comfort of the Lord that enables us to go forth, trusting Him for Godly results. You need not faint; you can pray.

As you pray you will find your disposition changing. Where doubt was found, faith will now exist. Your confidence will flourish, your prayers will be prayed with expectation as well as with joy. You need not faint, pray. Your victory is on the other side of your prayer.

Day 99

Psalm 109:115 Thy word is a lamp unto my feet, and a light unto my path.

Thought: I Need Not Stumble; God's Word Is My Light

Focus: God's Word Offers 20/20 Vision

Life has many twists and turns, as well as numerous obstacles. Endeavoring to maneuver in this challenging course without God's Word can prove devastating. David chose not to stumble; he followed God's Word. It provided him the light needed for a safe journey.

Walking without the benefit of God's Word is unwise. Following our own instincts without consulting God can lead us into troublesome areas. Become both a student and a follower of the Word of God. It will provide the necessary light in what would be otherwise dangerous terrain. You need not stumble; God's Word will provide you the needed light.

Day 100

Luke 17:14 And when he saw them, he said unto them, Go shew yourselves unto the priests. And it came to pass, that, as they went, they were cleansed.

Thought: Blessings Come to Those That Obey

Focus: Why Stand in Defeat When You Can Walk Into Victory

Ten lepers cried out to the Lord for mercy. They recognized that no one else could correct their condition. They put all their hope in Jesus. He, perhaps, caught them off guard, commanding them, yet as lepers, to go show themselves unto the priest. Having nothing to lose, they went and were healed.

When the Lord gives you directions that seem to make no sense, how do you respond? If it is God, obedience is essential. Though you might not understand the how or the why, God knows exactly what the outcome will be. Blessings follow those that obey.

Day 101

Acts 12:15 And they said unto her, Thou art mad. But she constantly affirmed that it was even so. Then said they, It is his angel.

Thought Don't Allow The Doubt Of Others To Quench Your Faith

Focus: Your Prayers Can Make the Difference

While Peter was bound in prison, the church prayed for his release. God honored their cries and sent an angel to deliver him. Upon his release, Peter went to where they had gathered for prayer. When he arrived, those that were praying were told that he was there. They declared that it was not possible and told the messenger that she was mad. She refused to allow their doubts to quench her faith. She knew that their prayers had made the difference.

As you go before the Lord in prayer, be assured that your prayers can make the difference. Others may doubt what is possible but their lack of faith cannot be allowed to quench your faith. As God moves on your behalf, remain assured that your prayers have made the difference.

Day 102

Luke 19:2-4 And, behold, there was a man named Zacchaeus, which was the chief among the publicans, and he was rich. And he sought to see Jesus who he was; and could not for the press, because he was little of stature. And he ran before, and climbed up into a sycomore tree to see him: for he was to pass that way.

Thought: Whatever It Might Take; See Jesus

Focus: Don't Wait For Tomorrow, Take Advantage Of Today

Zacchaeus was committed to seeing Jesus. He was determined that whatever it would take, he was going to see Jesus that day. Being short, he was unable to see the Master as he passed by, because of the crowd. Refusing to be denied and not knowing when he would get another chance, Zacchaeus ran ahead and climbed a tree. His efforts were not in vain, he saw Jesus that day.

As the Lord provides an opportunity for you to see Him, as you have never seen Him before, do not allow it to pass you by. Whatever effort it may take, whatever you must deny, be willing. The blessings that the Lord wants to pour into your life will be much greater than the price you are being asked to pay. Don't wait for tomorrow, take advantage of today.

Day 103

2 Corinthians 3:6 Who also hath made us able ministers of the new testament; not of the letter, but of the spirit: for the letter killeth, but the spirit giveth life.

Thought: Seek To Bless Not Simply Restrict

Focus: It Is The Spirit That Brings Life

As Apostle Paul responds to questions about his authority as an Apostle, he notes that he has been empowered by God to minister, not by the letter, but by the spirit. Those that minister must seek to bless not simply restrict. Emphasizing the letter results in death while being led by the spirit brings life.

A look at the life of Jesus provides multiple examples of how he blessed those he encountered. It was not with the law but with the spirit he brought folks into a relationship with God. Those that had been bound by the law were being set free.

Day 104

Exodus 14:22 And the children of Israel went into the midst of the sea upon the dry ground: and the waters were a wall unto them on their right hand, and on their left.

Thought: Your Way Of Deliverance Awaits You

Focus: Your Journey Has Been Prepared By God

When Israel thought they were trapped they cried cries of defeat unto the Lord. They could not see how they could cross this great sea. What they did not understand was that the Lord had prepared their journey. During their storm, He had prepared dry land for them. He simply spoke to the wind moving the sea, bringing about dry land for Israel to walk across. He was taking them to victory.

Your journey may appear too challenging for you to survive, but you need not doubt. Every step has been prepared by God. Stay focused on Him and walk in faith, knowing that your deliverance awaits you. Your "dry land" awaits you.

Day 105

Psalm 27:13-14 I had fainted, unless I had believed to see the goodness of the Lord in the land of the living. Wait on the Lord: be of good courage, and he shall strengthen thine heart: wait, I say, on the Lord.

Thought: Now Is Not The Time To Give Up

Focus: Your Waiting Will Be Rewarded

David acknowledges that he is facing great odds, odds that he recognizes that he by himself cannot overcome. During this challenge, he chooses not to faint, but to wait on the Lord. It is with great expectation that he places his trust in the Lord. As he waits, he finds comfort, as the Lord strengthens his heart. His waiting is rewarded.

The obstacles and challenges that a saint faces can be overwhelming. As you find yourself in that position, you need not allow yourself to be overcome with fear and anxiety. Place your confidence into the hands of the Lord and wait for His direction. As you stay focused on Him you will find strength to go forward. Now is not the time to give up; your waiting will be rewarded.

Day 106

Philippians 4:8 Finally, brethren, whatsoever things are true, whatsoever things are honest, whatsoever things are just, whatsoever things are pure, whatsoever things are lovely, whatsoever things are of good report; if there be any virtue, and if there be any praise, think on these things.

Thought: Your Thoughts Will Shape Your Behavior

Focus: Help Shape Your Future; Focus on The Positive

Thoughts are important; they have an impact on your behavior, as they help shape your attitude. Paul encourages us to think on those things of a good report. Those that look through a positive lens build a wall against doubt and negative thoughts. They open the door to faith and positive behavior.

Your thoughts matter; they create an attitude resulting in behavior. If you constantly look at life as negative, it will result in added doubt and anxiety. Stay focused on the positive and add to your faith and expectation. Thoughts matter; they shape your future.

Day 107

Philippians 4:6 Be careful for nothing; but in every thing by prayer and supplication with thanksgiving let your requests be made known unto God.

Thought: Pray With Confidence And Expectation

Focus: Present Your Requests With Thanksgiving

Paul provides us with instructions for prayer, emphasizing the importance of having a positive approach. Our petitions should not be presented with anxiety but rather with a spirit of thanksgiving. God awaits our requests, having the power and desire to bless.

What is in your spirit when you pray? Are you simply venting with no thoughts of receiving, or is there a high level of expectation? Let your prayers be without anxiety, maintaining a spirit of anticipation. It is God's desire to respond to your request.

Day 108

Isaiah 40:29 He giveth power to the faint; and to them that have no might he increaseth strength.

Thought: Knowing Where Your Help Comes from Is Key

Focus: God Is Your Provider

Isaiah speaks not only of a God that neither sleep or slumbers, but also of one who is aware of the frailty of man. It is in their weakest moments, as they look to Him, that He provides strength and might for their journey.

Each of us has limited strength. As we recognize this, and place our dependency on God, we become the recipients of the needed strength and might that He provides. The key is knowing where your strength comes from.

Day 109

Luke 9:42 And as he was yet a coming, the devil threw him down, and tare him. And Jesus rebuked the unclean spirit, and healed the child, and delivered him again to his father.

Thought: Satan May Seek to Fight, But Victory Is In The Hands Of Jesus

Focus: There May Be a Temporary Setback, But Victory Is Coming

A father had brought his son to be healed. A demon controlled the child, continuously causing him to be bruised. Jesus called for the child that he might heal him. As the child was coming, the demon attacked one last time. Jesus rebuked the unclean spirit and healed the child.

As you anticipate God's blessings flowing into your life, you may face a temporary setback. Satan, refusing to yield, will continue to seek to rob you of your faith. Refuse to compromise, knowing that victory is coming. Victory remains in the hands of Jesus.

Day 110

Luke 8:49-50 While he yet spake, there cometh one from the ruler of the synagogue's house, saying to him, Thy daughter is dead; trouble not the Master. But when Jesus heard it, he answered him, saying, Fear not: believe only, and she shall be made whole.

Thought: Maintain Your Faith; God's Promise Will Be Kept

Reflection for the Day: Your Faith Will Be Challenged

A father came to Jesus, requesting that the master come to his house that his daughter would be healed. Jesus agreed. As they traveled, word came that it was too late, the child had died. The father, knowing both what Jesus had promised and what he just heard, became confused. Realizing what was occurring, Jesus quickly told the man, be not afraid, believe only. His promise would be kept; his daughter would be healed.

When Jesus makes a promise he knows all that will yet take place. He is neither shocked or controlled by anything that may occur. It is at those times, when your faith is being challenged, that you must maintain your confidence. Even when matters go from bad to worse, God's promises will be kept.

Day 111

Acts 19:2 He said unto them, Have ye received the Holy Ghost since ye believed? And they said unto him, We have not so much as heard whether there be any Holy Ghost.

Thought: There Are Things Yet For You To Learn

Focus: Your Obedience Will Lead To Blessings

As Paul traveled to Ephesus, for the first time, he came across a group of believers. When asked if they had received the Holy Ghost, they acknowledged they had neither received or knew about the Holy Ghost. Hearing their response, Paul began to instruct them. Once hearing Paul, they were baptized and received the Holy Ghost. They realized, though they were believers, there were many things yet for them to learn. They responded with obedience and were blessed.

Regardless of what you currently know about the Lord there is always more to learn. Maintain a spirit that seeks to hear from the Lord. As the Spirit instructs you be obedient. His blessings will follow your obedience.

Day 112

Philippians 3:14 I press toward the mark for the prize of the high calling of God in Christ Jesus.

Thought: You May Not Be There Yet But Press Your Way

Reflection for the Day: The Mark Is Set; It Cannot Be Changed

Paul acknowledges in his writings that he has not reached the place in God that he desires. He notes that there is a mark, set by God, that he is determined to reach. There are obstacles but he is committed to press through them all.

There is a place in God's will that you desire to be in, but at times it may seem unreachable. Two things must be understood. First, the mark has been set by God and it cannot be adjusted. Second there will be obstacles, but if you press your way, you will arrive at your goal.

Day 113

Luke 1:38 And Mary said, Behold the handmaid of the Lord; be it unto me according to thy word. And the angel departed from her.

Thought: With or Without Your Understanding; God's Will Shall Be Accomplished

Focus: The Impossible Is Possible

As Mary listened to Gabriel telling her she was going to have a child, she understood not how that could be. When he told her that the Holy Ghost would overshadow her, she did not understand but declared, according to thy word. She yielded herself into the hands of the Lord.

As God reveals His will to you, some things may seem impossible. The key is knowing if it is of God or man. If it is of God, with or without understanding, yield yourself into the hands of the Lord. His will shall be accomplished.

Day 114

Luke 2:17 And when they had seen it, they made known abroad the saying which was told them concerning this child.

Thought: The Story Must Be Told

Focus: All Must Hear; No One Is To Be Left Out

The first evangelists were a group of shepherds. When they received word of the birth of Jesus, they made haste to go where he was. Once they worshipped him, they left to carry the message everywhere. It was a story that must be told. No one could be left out.

God has graciously revealed to you who He is. You have had the joy to worship and serve Him. As you enjoy your walk with Him, the message must be shared. What you now know, others must hear. No one is to be left out.

Day 115

Luke 2:19 But Mary kept all these things and pondered them in her heart.

Thought: There Is a Time to Share, There Is a Time To Quietly Give Thought

Focus: Quiet Is a Good Thing

In young Mary's life, much was taking place. She is in a manger, having just given birth. With her baby wrapped in swaddling clothes, a group of shepherds come to see the baby. After worshiping the "Christ child", they hurry off to tell all the birth of Jesus. In the midst of all that is occurring, Mary remains quiet. She is pondering all these things in her heart.

In the midst of the hand of God upon your life, before taking any action, it may be best to quietly give thought to all that is occurring. There is a time to share, and there is also a time to quietly give thought. Before taking action, be assured that you have a full grasp on what God is doing.

Day 116

Luke 2:40 And the child grew, and waxed strong in spirit, filled with wisdom: and the grace of God was upon him.

Thought: In All Of God's Creation Growth Is Present

Focus: Where There Is No Growth There Is No Life

The scripture speaks of the growth that took place in the life of young Jesus. He waxed strong in spirit and was filled with wisdom. In all of God's creation growth is present. Where there is no growth there is no life.

As you continue your walk in the Lord, growth must take place. Both spiritual and natural growth are a part of the process that occurs in the life of the believer. As you spend time with the Lord, your growth will become evident to all. No growth, no life.

Day 117

John 3:30 He must increase, but I must decrease.

Thought: We Must Decrease as Jesus Increases

Focus: Stay Focused on The Lord

John knew his assignment; he was the voice crying out in the wilderness. John's role was vital, he told all of the ones that came after him. John did not allow the attention he received to alter his awareness of who he was and who Jesus was. He must decrease as Jesus increased.

Every child of God is to play a part in the sharing of the gospel message. The key is to never lose focus of who Jesus is. As you are effectively used in your assignment, remember, you must decrease as Jesus increases.

Day 118

Luke 2:52 And Jesus increased in wisdom and stature, and in favour with God and man.

Thought: Growth Is an Ongoing Process

Focus: Position Yourself That You Might Gain from Others

At age twelve, Jesus left his parents and went into the Temple. It was there that he both listened and asked questions of the learned men. It was part of the process, as he increased in wisdom and stature, gaining favor with God and man.

Growth is essential in everyone's life. Position yourself that you might gain from others. Recognizing that growth is a process, maintain your commitment to consistent growth. You will grow daily, not in a day.

Day 119

1 Corinthians 11:28 But let a man examine himself, and so let him eat of that bread, and drink of that cup.

Thought: Examination Begins with Self

Focus: Change Is to Be the Result

In preparation for receiving the "Lord's Supper", we are instructed by Paul to examine ourselves. The focus is to be looking inward, with consideration being given to those areas that are not pleasing to the Lord. With a spirit of repentance, and a commitment to the needed changes, the saint should then eat and drink of the broken body and blood of the Lord.

Communion must not be allowed to simply become a ritual taken at a given time. It is to be a time when careful thought is given to our current walk with the Lord. As you examine yourself, consider where your actions or thoughts may not be pleasing to the Lord. It is with a repentant heart; you are to drink from the broken body and blood of the Lord.

Day 120

Luke 2:25-26 And, behold, there was a man in Jerusalem, whose name was Simeon; and the same man was just and devout, waiting for the consolation of Israel: and the Holy Ghost was upon him. And it was revealed unto him by the Holy Ghost, that he should not see death, before he had seen the Lord's Christ.

Thought: What The Spirit Reveals Will Take Place

Focus: God Not Only Knows Today, He Also Knows Tomorrow

Simeon was a just and devout man of God. It was revealed to him by the Holy Spirit, that he would not die, without first seeing the Christ child. As he served in his duties, he was led by the Spirit into the Temple, just as Joseph and Mary brought baby Jesus there to be blessed. What was revealed took place.

As you walk closely with the Lord, the Spirit will share with you. Be assured that what is revealed will take place. That includes what might appear to be impossible. God not only knows today, He knows tomorrow.

Day 121

Matthew 4:4 But he answered and said, It is written, Man shall not live by bread alone, but by every word that proceedeth out of the mouth of God.

Thought: Life Is Found In The Word Of God

Focus: Allow Not The Tempter To Deceive You

Jesus was led by the Spirit into the wilderness. After forty days of fasting, he hungered. It was at that time the tempter came to challenge him. "If thou be the son of God, turn these stones into bread," he challenged Jesus. The response was a Word response. "Man does not live by bread alone, but by every word that proceedeth out of the mouth of God." Life is found in the Word.

At your most challenging moments, the tempter will offer to meet your need. Your acceptance will move you outside the Word of God. It is essential, at those times, that you remain true to the Word. It is there you will find life.

Day 122

Luke 1:30-31 And the angel said unto her, Fear not, Mary: for thou hast found favour with God. And, behold, thou shalt conceive in thy womb, and bring forth a son, and shalt call his name JESUS.

Thought: God Has A Purpose For Your Life

Focus: Your Assignment Is Critical

Mary was certainly puzzled when she received Gabriel's directions for her life. She felt completely inadequate for her unique purpose, but yet when she recognized it was God's assignment for her life she declared," let it be according to thy word". She understood her assignment was critical; it must be fulfilled.

Each of God's children are given gifts and talents, all of which are to be used for the sake of the Kingdom. As you discover your role, it is essential that you understand that it is a critical assignment. Present yourself to the Lord and fulfill your role with a spirit of excellence.

Day 123

Luke 1:18 And Zacharias said unto the angel, whereby shall I know this? for I am an old man, and my wife well stricken in years.

Thought: With God There Are No Limits

Focus: There Is No Need to Doubt

Zacharias, when told that his prayer was heard, declared that it was not possible. He explained to the angel that both he and his wife were too old to have a child. Gabriel, when hearing Zacharias, rebuked him for his response. Nothing limits God to bless whom He chooses to bless.

Coming to a place when one understands that nothing limits God is essential. God's Word is not limited to any circumstance or time limits. When He speaks, there is no need to doubt; simply say thank you.

Day 124

Romans 8:31 What shall we then say to these things? If God be for us, who can be against us?

Thought: Your Walk In God Is Secure

Focus: God Has Your Back

The walk of the saint is secure. As they walk in obedience to God's Word, they have the assurance of knowing, no one has the power to stop them. There may be some bumps in the road but with God fighting for them, they cannot be defeated.

The enemy wants to defeat you, he desires to separate you from God. There will be battles, but as you stay focused on the Lord, be assured no one can separate you from the love of God. Your walk is secure, God has your back.

Day 125

Joshua 6:20 So the people shouted when the priests blew with the trumpets: and it came to pass, when the people heard the sound of the trumpet, and the people shouted with a great shout, that the wall fell down flat, so that the people went up into the city, every man straight before him, and they took the city.

Thought: Obedience Precedes Victory

Focus: What You Do Not Understand; God Does

Joshua was given detailed directions for how the people of Israel would approach Jericho. They were to march around the walls once for six days and then on the seventh day, seven times. Each time they marched around they were to remain silent until the final time, when upon hearing the sound of the trumpet, they were to shout a great shout. As they obeyed, they watched as the Lord brought the walls down flat. Their obedience preceded their victory.

There will be times that the directions the Lord gives you may not seem logical. How you respond is key. It is through your obedience that you will experience victory. God knows exactly why He is leading you in the manner that He is. Be assured, what you don't understand, He does.

Day 126

Luke 15:17-19 And when he came to himself, he said, How many hired servants of my fathers have bread enough and to spare, and I perish with hunger! I will arise and go to my father, and will say unto him, Father, I have sinned against heaven, and before thee, And am no more worthy to be called thy son: make me as one of thy hired servants.

Thought: Change Begins When One Accepts Who They Truly Are

Focus: The Lord Awaits Your Arrival

With money in his pocket, this man forgot who he was and his dependency on his father. It took the loss of all his possessions and his "friends" to help remember who he was. As he came to himself, change began. With a humble and repentant heart, he returned to his father. He quickly learned that his father awaited his return.

At different levels, we are vulnerable to forgetting just how frail we are and the importance of understanding our dependency on God. Don't wait for disaster to strike, remind yourself constantly of your need to depend on God. If you have drifted at all, be aware the Lord awaits your arrival. He holds your blessings in His hands.

Day 127

Proverbs 15:1 A soft answer turneth away wrath: but grievous words stir up anger.

Thought: Choose Them Carefully; Your Words Matter

Focus: Are You Taking Responsibility for Your Words

We often speak without giving thought to the impact of our words. The impact is even greater during times of conflict where a soft answer has the ability to turn away wrath, while a grievous response will easily result in greater anger. We must take responsibility for our words understanding they have power.

As a child of God, you have the privilege of being a blessing to others. There will be times that you will be called upon to relinquish your feelings for the sake of others. In every conversation choose your words wisely, knowing you have power to add value to the conversation. Your words matter.

Day 128

1 Peter 1:14-15 As obedient children, not fashioning yourselves according to the former lusts in your ignorance: But as he which hath called you is holy, so be ye holy in all manner of conversation;

Thought: With Knowledge Comes Change

Focus: You Have Been Called To Be Holy

Prior to coming into the knowledge of Jesus, our lives were lived in a manner that was not pleasing to Him. Through the learning we received, our entire conversation was to change. No longer being led by our former lust, our lives were now to be holy. We were called by a holy God that we too might be holy.

As you look back at your life, prior to following the Lord, you will note that you were being fashioned, in ignorance, by your former lusts. With a spirit of obedience, you now are led by the teachings of the Lord. Your commitment, as a child of God, is to live a holy life. As He is holy, you also desire to be holy.

Day 129

Colossians 3:13 Forbearing one another, and forgiving one another, if any man have a quarrel against any: even as Christ forgave you, so also do ye.

Thought: Godliness Includes Forgiveness

Focus: As God Forgave Us; We Must Forgive One Another

In Paul's teaching, we are instructed of the necessity of forgiving one another. Disagreements take place in everyday life which can result in great animosity, if not properly handled. What is necessary is a spirit to forgive. Godliness includes forgiveness.

You will, at times in your life, find yourself in a dispute with others. In most times, there is blame on both sides. What is necessary for all involved is a spirit to forgive. As God forgave you, you must be ready to forgive others.

Day 130

James 4:6 But he giveth more grace. Wherefore he saith, God resisteth the proud, but giveth grace unto the humble.

Thought: God's Grace Is Essential

Focus: It Is the Humble That Receive "More Grace"

We live in a corrupt world that can have an impact on every child of God. While the proud are vulnerable, God's grace is provided to the humble. It is through the grace of God that the humble can remain true to God's Word. Humility is essential.

One's dependency on God is evident in every aspect of life. This includes our walk in a corrupt world. It is essential that you remain humble, knowing that your strength comes not from self, but from the Lord. It is the humble saint that receives more grace, allowing him to go forward in God.

Day 131

Joshua 10:8 And the Lord said unto Joshua, Fear them not: for I have delivered them into thine hand; there shall not a man of them stand before thee.

Thought: Your Enemy Has Already Been Defeated

Focus: Go Forth With Confidence

After hearing that Gibeon had entered into a league with Israel, the five kings of the Amorites sought to make war with them. Responding to their request, Joshua gathered his men to assist Gibeon. As they prepared, God spoke to Joshua. "Fear them not, for I have delivered them into your hand". Their enemy had already been defeated, they could go forth with confidence.

As you journey in the will of God, there will be times that you face those that will seek to come against you. When this occurs, you need not fear, for God has already placed them into your hand. Simply go forth with confidence, victory has been assured.

Day 132

John 4:13-14 Jesus answered and said unto her, Whosoever drinketh of this water shall thirst again: But whosoever drinketh of the water that I shall give him shall never thirst; but the water that I shall give him shall be in him a well of water springing up into everlasting life.

Thought: God's Blessings Do Not Lose Their Power; They Last Forever

Focus: Receive What God Has Prepared For You; You Shall Be Blessed

In the conversation Jesus had with the Samaritan woman, he spoke of the water that he had to offer. He explained that the water that came from the well would provide only temporary relief, while those that drank the water he offered, would thirst no more. God's blessings last forever.

If you are not careful, your search will focus on natural blessings. As your attention remains on those things, you will be overlooking what God has to offer. Natural blessings satisfy only for a short time, while God's last forever.

Day 133

Genesis 15:1 After these things the word of the LORD came unto Abram in a vision, saying, Fear not, Abram: I am thy shield, and thy exceeding great reward.

Thought: There Is No Need To Fear

Focus: God Will Both Protect And Provide

After defeating, through God's help, the armies that had taken Lot captive, Abram refused to accept anything from the King of Sodom for his help. Abram's dependence remained solely on God. He accepted the fact that God was both his protector and his provider.

When the Lord, in a vision, told Abram he was his shield and his great reward, he was sharing his commitment to all that trust him. As you walk in obedience to God's Word, you have no need to fear. He will both protect and provide for you.

Day 134

Hebrews 6:15 And so, after he had patiently endured, he obtained the promise.

Thought: Wait Patiently, You Will Not Be Disappointed

Focus: God's Timing Is Not Man's

God made a promise to Abraham, he would bless him and multiply him. The promise was fulfilled, but not before many years past filled with many challenges. Throughout all those years, Abraham continued to look to the Lord. His faith was not diminished nor without reward. After he patiently endured, he received the promise.

Every promise God makes will be fulfilled. What must be understood is that the Lord's timing is different than man's timing. With patience, endure all that is before you. As you continue to grow, while you wait, your walk with God will become closer. Stay focused on Him, you will not be disappointed

Day 135

Nehemiah 2:1 And it came to pass in the month Nisan, in the twentieth year of Artaxerxes the king, that wine was before him: and I took up the wine, and gave it unto the king. Now I had not been beforetime sad in his presence.

Thought: Your Prayer May Not Be Fulfilled Today But There Is A Tomorrow

Focus: God Determines When And How

In chapter one, we read how Nehemiah petitioned the Lord praying and fasting certain days. The fact that he did not receive a response quickly did not stop the man of God. He remained before the Lord, continuing to cry out. His answer did not come the first day but there was a tomorrow. God chose the time and the how.

When God puts a prayer into your spirit be assured, He will respond. Your answer may not come quickly, but there is a tomorrow. He will determine when and how, but your answer will come.

Day 136

Hebrews 12:1 Wherefore seeing we also are compassed about with so great a cloud of witnesses, let us lay aside every weight, and the sin which doth so easily beset us, and let us run with patience the race that is set before us.

Thought: As Others Ran Before Us; So Must We Run

Focus: All Hindrances Must Go

The preceding chapter, often called the faith chapter, presents a hosts of men and women that walked by faith. They set an example for us to follow. The author exhorts us to lay aside all hindrances, and with patience, run the race that is set before us.

God has set before you a race that you are to run. That it might be a successful run, it is essential that you lay aside every hindrance, and with patience, run your race. As others ran before you, it is your time to run.

Day 137

1 Samuel 15:22 And Samuel said, Hath the LORD as great delight in burnt offerings and sacrifices, as in obeying the voice of the LORD? Behold, to obey is better than sacrifice, and to hearken than the fat of rams.

Thought: Obedience Is Not Optional

Focus: Nothing Can Take Its Place

Upon giving the Israelites, the victory over the Amalekites, God instructed Saul to kill all of the spoil. Saul chose not to obey what the Lord had told him, but rather offer a portion of the sheep and oxen to the Lord as a sacrifice. He was quickly rebuked. Obedience is not optional. There can be no substitutes.

As God instructs you, it is essential that you obey. There is nothing you can choose to do that will please the Lord other than what He has instructed you to do. Obedience is not optional; it requires complete adherence.

Day 138

Psalm 111:10 The fear of the LORD is the beginning of wisdom: a good understanding have all they that do his commandments: his praise endureth forever.

Thought: There Is One True Source Of Wisdom; God

Focus: Obedience Must Follow Recognition

The author helps us to understand the source of wisdom. It begins with our reverence and honor of who God is. As we walk in His ways, we gain an understanding of why He leads us in the manner that He does. Our praises for who He is will follow.

It is the Lord's desire that His children walk in wisdom. This begins with a reverence for who He is. As you honor Him and walk in His Word, you will gain a greater understanding of who He is. Your praises will be offered with a deeper recognition of who He is.

Day 139

Colossians 3:9 Lie not one to another, seeing that ye have put off the old man with his deeds.

Thought: The Old Must Die That the New Might Live

Focus: What Was Accepted Yesterday Is No Longer Today

The chapter helps us to understand the necessity of putting aside yesterday's early behavior. What was accepted, before we knew the Lord, is to be no longer a part of our lives. The old man must be put aside that the new might live.

As you now seek to follow the Lord, have you properly put aside the "old man"? It is essential that those things that you once accepted are no longer a part of who you are now. Those that follow Christ must walk uprightly before him. You are now a new creature.

Day 140

Luke 6:12-16 And it came to pass in those days, that he went out into a mountain to pray, and continued all night in prayer to God. And when it was day, he called unto him his disciples: and of them he chose twelve, whom also he named apostles; Simon, (whom he also named Peter,) and Andrew his brother, James and John, Philip and Bartholomew, Matthew and Thomas, James the son of Alphaeus, and Simon called Zelotes, And Judas the brother of James, and Judas Iscariot, which also was the traitor.

Thought: Before Deciding, Pray

Focus: The Greater The Decision; The More Prayer Is Needed

Jesus was about to make a vital decision; the choosing of the twelve. Understanding the importance of the decision, he spent the night in prayer. It was only then that his decision was made. Prayer preceded his decision.

Rushing into making decisions is unwise. Wisdom instructs us to first approach God. As decisions arise, first spend time in prayer. As you pray, the Spirit will direct you in the proper direction. Always insist on prayer preceding the making of your decision.

Day 141

2 Corinthians 10:4 (For the weapons of our warfare are not carnal, but mighty through God to the pulling down of strong holds;).

Thought: You Have Been Equipped to Win

Focus: Weapons Not Used Have No Power

Paul reminds us that we are in a spiritual warfare, one that cannot be won using non-spiritual weapons. We have been equipped with weapons that are mighty; prayer, fasting, and the Word of God. When applied, with faith, we can bring down strongholds. It is essential that they do not remain idle, they must be used.

As a child of God, you have been equipped with weapons of power. Unfortunately, many do not put them to use. It is essential that you maintain a prayer life, with quality time spent in the Word. Add fasting to the equation and you will discover the ability, through God, to the pulling down of strongholds.

Day 142

Proverbs 16:7 When a man's ways please the LORD, he maketh even his enemies to be at peace with him.

Thought: The Key Is Pleasing God

Focus: Stay Focused on Pleasing God, The Rest Is In His Hands

Pleasing God is the key to a blessed life. All the various challenges one might face, including one's enemies, are under His control. No matter what the enemy might seek to do, God will make him be at peace with you. Success comes when the focus remains on pleasing God.

Under the stress of dealing with one's enemy, focus on pleasing God can be lost. This is unfortunate. Success is maintained when you realize, that when you please God, He will make even your enemy to be at peace with you. Allow no one to distract you, stay focused on God.

Day 143

John 6:9 There is a lad here, which hath five barley loaves, and two small fishes: but what are they among so many?

Thought: Your Little Is All God Needs

Focus: Present What You Have to Jesus; He Will Do the Rest

Jesus, seeing the need of the multitude to eat, asked what was available to feed them. Phillip responded that they did not have sufficient money to buy the needed bread. He added that there was a lad with five loaves and two fish, but that was not able to meet the need of so many. Jesus instructed them to give him the bread and fish. He then had the multitude to sit, he gave thanks, and proceeded to feed all. Our little is all God needs.

You may feel that you don't have sufficient resources to meet your own needs, or perhaps to bless others. The key is presenting what you do have to Jesus. Your little is all he needs.

Day 144

1 Thessalonians 5:11 Wherefore comfort yourselves together, and edify one another, even as also ye do.

Thought: You Have the Power To Comfort One Another

Focus: Take Responsibility to Bless Those in Your Midst

As we celebrate what God has done for us, let us not overlook the importance of encouraging one another. In each of our lives, when challenging times do occur, a kind word can help so much. You have the power with that word or kind gesture to bless. Take responsibility to add value to the lives of those in your midst. You can be the difference maker.

No one goes through life without challenging times. As you interact with others, always seek to encourage. You have the privilege and opportunity to add value to those in your midst. Your kind words or gesture can make the difference in your brother's or sister's life. Comfort one another.

Day 145

Luke 21:3-4 And he said, Of a truth I say unto you, that this poor widow hath cast in more than they all: For all these have of their abundance cast in unto the offerings of God: but she of her penury hath cast in all the living that she had.

Thought: It Is Not The Amount That Matters

Focus: How Much Of You Are You Giving?

The Word of God encourages us to be liberal givers. It does not measure liberality by the amount, but by the spirit in which it is given. Jesus comments to this by contrasting those that are rich, who give of their abundance, with a poor widow who gave all that she had. Her gift is much smaller in amount but greater in spirit. She has given all of herself.

Giving is not limited to finance. It includes not only our treasure but also our time and talent. In each of these areas the spirit of how you give is measured more than the amount. As you give thought to your level of giving, consider if you are giving of your abundance or are you a sacrificial giver? How much of you are you giving?

Day 146

Psalm 19:1 The heavens declare the glory of God; and the firmament sheweth his handywork.

Thought: Creation Speaks of His Power

Focus: The Evidence Is Overwhelming

Several years ago we flew over the Rocky Mountains. Looking at His handiwork, I struggled to see how anyone could doubt His existence. Only God, with His unlimited power, could create such a masterpiece. His creation declares who He is.

There are unlimited signs that declare the existence of God. If you ever wrestle with doubt, simply look at His creation. The heavens declare His glory, and the firmament His handiwork. The evidence is overwhelming.

Day 147

1 Peter 5:7 Casting all your care upon him; for he careth for you.

Thought: What You Cannot Handle, God Can

Focus: What Impacts You Is His Concern

Anxiety is a powerful weapon that the enemy uses against the people of God. Unfortunately, the privilege of releasing those situations that are too great for us, to the Lord is not taken advantage of. This results in anxiety which can overcome the child of God. The key is casting our cares upon Him. What is too great for us, He can handle.

Do you find yourself burdened down with situations that are too great for you to handle? You need not. Cast all your cares upon Him. All that impacts you is a concern of His. He has the power to fix what you are not able to do.

Day 148

Romans 12:2 And be not conformed to this world: but be ye transformed by the renewing of your mind, that ye may prove what is that good, and acceptable, and perfect, will of God.

Thought: You Have Something To Prove

Focus: Be Not Conformed, Be Transformed

Paul exhorts us to live our lives that others might see God's will being demonstrated. We cannot be conformed to this world, but must be transformed by the renewing of our minds. We have something to prove.

You have the joy and responsibility of demonstrating a life that presents who Jesus is. As you give yourself to a total transformation, you will be proving what is the good, and acceptable, and perfect will of God.

Day 149

James 4:7 Submit yourselves therefore to God. Resist the devil, and he will flee from you.

Thought: Victory Begins with Submission

Focus: The Humble Are Recipients of God's Grace

A battle exists within us. The spirit of envy that exists in us, wrestles with our desire to please God. Victory occurs, as with humility, submission to the Lord takes place. There is then the ability to resist the devil causing him to flee. Victory begins with submission.

Within everyone, who seeks to follow God, a spirit that lusteth to envy is present. Your victory begins as you totally submit yourself into the hands of the Lord. As you humbly present yourself before Him, you will be a recipient of His grace empowering you to resist the devil. Your victory begins as you submit.

Day 150

Ecclesiastes 4:9-10 Two are better than one because a good return comes when two work together. If one of them falls, the other can help him up. But who will help the pitiful person who falls down alone?

Thought: There Is Safety in Numbers

Focus: Be Prepared to Assist Your Brother

We have been wisely taught; one is an insignificant number to achieve greatness. There is wisdom in recognizing that two are better than one. There is always a chance of one falling. The other needs to be able to help him up. There is safety in numbers.

As you go forth to accomplish things for the Lord, take note of the wisdom of not going forth by yourself. No matter your strength, no one is beyond the possibility of falling. If that time might come, consider the importance of having another with you in a position to pick you up. There is safety in numbers.

Day 151

1 Peter 2:9 But ye are a chosen generation, a royal priesthood, an holy nation, a peculiar people; that ye should shew forth the praises of him who hath called you out of darkness into his marvellous light.

Thought: You Have Been Called To Demonstrate God's Goodness

Focus: Some Praises Are Spoken, Others Are Lived

As children of the Lord, we must understand our calling. We are to live that others might see the Lord through us. It is proper that we speak of the goodness of the Lord, but it is through our actions that we can fully declare who He is. We have been called to demonstrate His goodness.

God has called you to live a life that others might see the goodness of the Lord. Recognizing that your behavior speaks louder than your words, commit yourself to a Godly life. Take joy in revealing who the Lord is when words are not enough.

Day 152

Ephesians 6:12 For we wrestle not against flesh and blood, but against principalities, against powers, against the rulers of the darkness of this world, against spiritual wickedness in high places.

Thought: A Spiritual Battle Requires Spiritual Armor

Focus: Do You Know Who You Are Wrestling With?

The child of God must understand who he is wrestling against. His opponent is not flesh and blood, but the rulers of darkness of this world. To defeat this enemy, it requires being equipped with spiritual armor. It is only by the power of the Lord that victory can be obtained.

You are in a spiritual battle. You are not wrestling against flesh and blood, but a spiritual force. You will not defeat this enemy with your own power but must put on the whole armor of God. As you wrap yourself in the power of the Lord, you will be able to obtain victory. A spiritual battle requires spiritual armor.

Day 153

Mark 10:43-44 But so shall it not be among you: but whosoever will be great among you, shall be your minister: And whosoever of you will be the chiefest, shall be servant of all.

Thought: Seek To Serve Not To Be Served

Focus: Those That Are Great Display Their Greatest in Servanthood

The Lord's disciples, as his departure neared, began to scramble to assume the leadership of their group. Their approach was what would be considered appropriate in today's world's system. As Jesus knowing their desires, shared with them the Godly approach to leadership. Those that seek greatness in God must give themselves to servanthood.

Living in today's society provides a paradigm that is contrary to the ways of the Lord. As you seek to be used by the Lord, it is essential that you keep a servant's spirit and heart. Your focus must be on serving, not on being served. Your greatness will be displayed in how well you serve others.

Day 154

Ecclesiastes 7:3 Sorrow is better than laughter: for by the sadness of the countenance the heart is made better.

Thought: In The Midst of Your Tears, You Are Being Matured

Focus: Your Spiritual Maturity Occurs Greater During Times of Sadness Than Laughter

Solomon speaks of the importance of spiritual maturity, as he refers to the heart being made better. It is through sorrow, not laughter, that this growth comes about. Though we seek to avoid sorrow, it is where our greatest growth takes place.

As you examine your life, you will note that your greatest periods of growth took place during times of sorrow. As you go forward, recognize that the most challenging times of your life will include the maturity of your heart. Through your disappointment, your heart is being made better.

Day 155

Proverbs 3:11-12 My son, despise not the chastening of the LORD; neither be weary of his correction: For whom the LORD loveth he correcteth. even as a father the son in whom he delighteth.

Thought: Chastening Is Not A Bad Thing

Focus: A Closer Walk Awaits You

Solomon helps us to understand the intent of God's chastising. His correction comes to those that He loves that they might make any needed adjustments, bringing them to a closer walk with Him. With an understanding of the reasons for the correction, one has no reason to despise His chastisement. He chastises whom He loves.

The natural man finds no pleasure in chastisement. As a follower of Christ, it is important that you understand the intent of God as He corrects you. It is those that He loves who are the recipients, as He endeavors to bring them closer to Him. As you are corrected, make the needed adjustments, and draw closer to the one that loves you.

Day 156

Ecclesiastes 5:2 Be not rash with thy mouth, and let not thine heart be hasty to utter any thing before God: for God is in heaven, and thou upon earth: therefore let thy words be few.

Thought: God Knows All Things; We Know So Little

Focus: Listening Offers Greater Value Than Speaking

Solomon cautions us about speaking too quickly, as well as too often. Unfortunately, an excess of words is often uttered by the unwise without regard to the one that knows all. Wisdom teaches us that listening is of greater value than speaking.

Throughout scripture we are taught the importance of being a listener. Commit yourself to being one that hears; give yourself to hearing both the Lord and other people rather than speaking too quickly. Remind yourself, that while God knows everything, we know so little.

Day 157

Matthew 11:4-5 Jesus answered and said unto them, Go and shew John again those things which ye do hear and see: The blind receive their sight, and the lame walk, the lepers are cleansed, and the deaf hear, the dead are raised up, and the poor have the gospel preached to them.

Thought: The Facts Speak Clearly Of The Truth

Focus: When Doubt Attacks Give Thought To What You See

With John in prison, his life is about to come to a tragic end, he sent his disciples to question Jesus. They were to ask the Master if he was truly the Christ or should they wait for another. Jesus responded by telling John of all that was being done. The facts spoke clearly of the truth.

There will be in the midst of your journey, times that doubt will seek to overshadow you. At those times, give thought to what you have witnessed that Jesus has accomplished. The healings, and the many that have been delivered, clearly declare who Jesus is. The facts speak loudly of the truth.

Day 158

Matthew 6:33 But seek ye first the kingdom of God, and his righteousness; and all these things shall be added unto you.

Thought: Seek The Spiritual; God Will Add The Natural

Focus: Walk By Faith; You Will Not Be Disappointed

Where one's focus is, is key to their walk with God. Jesus instructs his followers to seek the kingdom of God. He assures them that as they seek spiritual things, God will add the natural things. They will not do without. Their faith will not be disappointed.

Your focus is key to your future. As you seek spiritual things, God will supply you with the natural things. Your faith will be honored, providing you testimony of a God that is true to His Word. You will not be disappointed.

Day 159

Proverbs 26:20 Where no wood is, there the fire goeth out: so where there is no talebearer, the strife ceaseth.

Thought: Your Silence Will Result in Peace

Focus: Be Not Quick to Share All That You Hear; Prayer Is A Better Option

Without fuel there is no fire. This is true with both wood and tale bearing. Solomon reminds us of the importance of not carrying to others everything that is heard. Through one's silence the fuel to keep it burning is taken away. We must not be quick to share all we hear. It would be better to pray.

God has called us to be peacemakers. It is essential that we understand the opportunity we must protect others from emotional attacks. Everything we hear is not to be shared. You have the option to take the fuel from a fire simply through your silence. Your better option is to pray.

Day 160

Joshua 14:12 Now therefore give me this mountain, whereof the Lord spake in that day; for thou heardest in that day how the Anakims were there, and that the cities were great and fenced: if so be the Lord will be with me, then I shall be able to drive them out, as the Lord said.

Thought: Don't Limit What God Has For You

Focus: With Faith And Obedience Stay Focused

Forty-five years is a long time to wait on a promise to be fulfilled. It becomes even more challenging when those around you are murmurous and complainers, but that was what Caleb faced. With all this against him, he yet remained focused on God and what he had been promised. Even when Joshua adjusted his faith, Caleb remained stern. He insisted on the promised mountain and possessed it. He would not limit God.

All of God's promises are not fulfilled immediately, even when you demonstrate faith. Knowing what God has promised, stay focused on Him and His ability to bless. The doubts of others, and the time you wait, cannot be allowed to impact your expectation. Insist on your mountain, you will possess it.

Day 161

Luke 6:12 And it came to pass in those days, that he went out into a mountain to pray, and continued all night in prayer to God.

Thought: Pray First, Then Act

Focus: Seek God's decision; He Will Direct

The scripture tells us that Jesus went into the mountain to pray. After spending the night in prayer, he called his disciples to him. From that group he chose twelve to be his apostles. He prayed first, then acted. Through prayer poor decisions can be avoided.

Constantly, we must make decisions that will impact our lives as well as others. It is key that before you make that decision, that you spend quality time in prayer. Allow the Lord to lead you that the proper decision is made. Pray first, then act.

Day 162

1 Samuel 1:13-15 Now Hannah, she spake in her heart; only her lips moved, but her voice was not heard: therefore Eli thought she had been drunken. And Eli said unto her, How long wilt thou be drunken? put away thy wine from thee. And Hannah answered and said, No, my lord, I am a woman of a sorrowful spirit: I have drunk neither wine nor strong drink, but have poured out my soul before the Lord.

Thought: Pray Like It Matters, God Will Respond.

Focus: If Your Prayer Doesn't Move You, Why Should It Move God?

Year after year, Hannah petitioned the Lord for a child. Each year that her request was not granted she was disappointed, but nothing could stop her prayer. With fervency, she cried out. Hannah's request meant too much to her to be deterred. Her determination was rewarded. Hannah gave birth to Samuel.

How much does your request mean to you? If it doesn't matter much to you, why should it matter to God. With determination, and expectation, pour out your soul before the Lord. Pray like it matters, God will respond.

Day 163

John 8:11 She said, No man, Lord. And Jesus said unto her, neither do I condemn thee: go, and sin no more.

Thought: Once Forgiven Change Must Occur

Focus: True Repentance Brings Forth A Change

The Jews came to Jesus demanding punishment for a woman caught in the act of adultery. To their disappointment, Jesus instead offered forgiveness. Included in forgiveness, he commanded the woman to "sin no more". A change in her behavior must occur.

We serve a forgiving God; one that is long suffering during our shortcomings. As you are grateful for His grace, you must not forget that He is also a Holy God. Let your acceptance of His forgiveness make you determined to live a life pleasing to Him.

Day 164

Proverbs 18:16 A man's gift maketh room for him, and bringeth him before great men.

Thought: Stay Focused on God; Your Gift Will Open the Proper Doors

Focus: God Intends for Your Gift to Be Used

In endeavoring to be elevated, people utilize many avenues. Political tactics as well as self-promoting are two of the ways often used. None are needed. As one stays focused on God, He will open every necessary door. He intends for the gifts, He has given, to be put into practice.

God has given you a gift that He intends for you to use. You need to do nothing other than to stay focused on Him and develop your gift. He will open all the necessary doors.

Day 165

Hebrews 10:35-37 Cast not away therefore your confidence, which hath great recompence of reward. For ye have need of patience, that, after ye have done the will of God, ye might receive the promise. For yet a little while, and he that shall come will come, and will not tarry.

Thought: Now Is Not the Time To Doubt

Focus: Your Patience Is About to Pay Off

Confidence, patience, and obedience are all essential qualities in the life of the child of God. Paul exhorts his readers not to allow challenging times to strip them of their confidence. As they commit themselves to fulfilling God's will, while waiting patiently for the Lord to act, they will not be disappointed. His promises will flow into their lives,

A healthy productive relationship with the Lord begins with knowing His will for your life. As you understand His direction for your life, and the promises He has made to you, there is less chance of error. With a patient spirit you can seek to please Him, knowing at His directed time, the promises will be fulfilled.

Day 166

Deuteronomy 6:5 And thou shalt love the LORD thy God with all thine heart, and with all thy soul, and with all thy might.

Thought: Complete Love Includes Emotions, Thoughts, And Strength

Focus: Nothing Less Is Acceptable

As Moses spoke with the people of Israel, he talked of the complete love that God commanded. A love that includes emotions, thoughts, and strength is what Moses spoke of. Nothing less is acceptable.

What part of your life is focused on God? Is He the recipient of your total love? He expects your complete love, heart, soul, and might. Nothing less is acceptable.

Day 167

Joshua 14:12 Now therefore give me this mountain, whereof the Lord spake in that day; for thou heardest in that day how the Anakims were there, and that the cities were great and fenced: if so be the Lord will be with me, then I shall be able to drive them out, as the Lord said.

Thought: Don't Limit What God Has For You

Focus: With Faith And Obedience Stay Focused

Forty-five years is a long time to wait on a promise to be fulfilled. It becomes even more challenging when those around you are murmurous and complainers, but that was what Caleb faced. With all this against him, he yet remained focused on God and what he had been promised. Even when Joshua adjusted his faith, Caleb remained stern. He insisted on the promised mountain and possessed it. He would not limit God.

All of God's promises are not fulfilled immediately, even when you demonstrate faith. Knowing what God has promised, stay focused on Him and His ability to bless. The doubts of others, and the time you wait, cannot be allowed to impact your expectation. Insist on your mountain, you will possess it.

Day 168

Proverbs 15:32 He that refuseth instruction despiseth his own soul: but he that heareth reproof getteth understanding.

Thought: The Unwise Refuse Instruction

Focus: Understanding Awaits You

Solomon helps us to understand the importance of receiving corrections. It is through reproof that proper adjustments can be made to one's actions. It is the unwise that refuses instruction.

In each of our lives there are areas that would benefit from the counsel of others. It may come as instruction or as reproof. As a person of wisdom, be quick to receive it and make the needed adjustments.

Day 169

Matthew 21:13 And said unto them, It is written, My house shall be called the house of prayer; but ye have made it a den of thieves.

Thought: God's House Is a House Of Prayer

Focus: It Must Not Be Defiled

As Jesus went into the Temple and saw the money changers and those selling doves, his response was immediate. He drove them out, declaring that his father's house is a house of prayer and they had turned it into a den of thieves. God's house must not be deviled.

Our attitude and behavior in God's house cannot be allowed to lose its importance. It is a house of prayer, a place where we reverence God and can come before Him in prayer. It must never be allowed to be defiled.

Day 170

Psalm 18:6 In my distress I called upon the LORD, and cried unto my God: he heard my voice out of his temple, and my cry came before him, even into his ears.

Thought: In The Midst Of Distress Call On The Lord; Let Your Cry Be Heard

Focus: He Will Respond

In every life, times of distress take place. They can cause one not to know how to respond. David provides the answer, call upon the Lord. He knew as he cried, God would hear and respond. His deliverance was on the way.

Allow no situation to defeat you. There will be times of distress but no situation is too great for God. Call upon Him. Let your cry be heard, He will respond.

Day 171

1 Peter 5:10 But the God of all grace, who hath called us unto his eternal glory by Christ Jesus, after that ye have suffered a while, make you perfect, stablish, strengthen, settle you.

Thought: There Is A Purpose For Your Time Of Suffering

Focus: You Are Being Perfected For God's Use

Suffering is not something we ask for or take joy in when it comes upon us. As much as we seek to avoid suffering, it is used by God to prepare us for His purpose. It is there to result in us being strengthened and stablished for the sake of others being blessed.

Before you cry out for any suffering you may be enduring to end, it is essential that you understand its purpose. God, through the suffering, is perfecting you. You are being established for the purpose of His will. Allow the settling process to take place that you may be ready to be used that others might be blessed.

Day 172

1 Peter 4:10 As every man hath received the gift, even so minister the same one to another, as good stewards of the manifold grace of God.

Thought: God Has Given You A Gift; It Must Be Used

Focus: Discover, Dedicate, Develop

Each child of God is the recipient of a gift from Him. It is given to be used to minister to others. It is important that the recipient understands that he does not choose the gift, but rather he discovers what God has given. It must then be dedicated to God and continuously developed.

You have been given a gift by God to be used to bless others. To properly impact the lives of others, you must be functioning in the right area. This begins by you, through prayer and counsel, discovering your gift. Recognizing that your gift must be dedicated to God, you must continue to grow it. You are a part of God's plan that all might be blessed.

Day 173

Luke 21:12-13 But before all these, they shall lay their hands on you, and persecute you, delivering you up to the synagogues, and into prisons, being brought before kings and rulers for my name's sake. And it shall turn to you for a testimony.

Thought: Today's Challenge Will Be Tomorrow's Testimony

Focus: With God You Will Not Be Defeated

As the disciples of Jesus were sent out to share the gospel, they were told of the attacks that they would face. In the midst of being told of the challenges, they were reminded that they did not need to lose hope. What they faced today would become tomorrow's testimony.

As you seek to live in accordance to the will of God, challenges will come. When they do, you need not lose hope. No matter what the enemy might throw at you, you have God on your side. With Him, you cannot be defeated. Today's challenge will be tomorrow's testimony.

Day 174

Luke 21:14-15 Settle it therefore in your hearts, not to meditate before what ye shall answer: For I will give you a mouth and wisdom, which all your adversaries shall not be able to gainsay nor resist.

Thought: Wait On The Lord, He Will Give You What To Say

Focus: God's Truth Cannot Be Refuted

Jesus wanted his disciples to know what they would encounter as they spread the gospel. They were going to face great opposition, some would be persecuted, others placed into prison. When they did come under attack, they were not to give thought to what they should say. The Lord would give them the proper words, words that could not be refuted.

Your warfare is not carnal, it is spiritual. As you go forth to tell others about the Lord, you will face opposition. Do not be quick to respond. Wait on the Lord, He will give you the words to say. They will be words that cannot be refuted.

Day 175

James 1:22 But be ye doers of the word, and not hearers only, deceiving your own selves.

Thought: It Is the Doing, Not The Hearing That Makes The Difference

Focus: Are You Deceiving Yourself?

While there are benefits to the hearing of God's Word, all of them are lost if there is no doing. Unfortunately, many deceive themselves with the belief that they are following the Lord while their actions declare otherwise. It is essential that we recognize that the power comes from the doing, not the hearing.

Is your life consistent with the teachings of the Lord? As you read and hear God's Word, let it be what guides your behavior. Do not simply be a hearer, be a doer of the Word. His blessings will follow.

Day 176

Luke 6:35 But love ye your enemies, and do good, and lend, hoping for nothing again; and your reward shall be great, and ye shall be the children of the Highest: for he is kind unto the unthankful and to the evil.

Thought: Love Others As God Loves Us

Focus: Your Goodness Can Overcome Evil

Jesus challenged his listeners to reach beyond their past responses. They were told to love not simply their friends, but also their enemies. They were to lend, not looking to receive back. They were to maintain kindness to the unthankful, knowing that their goodness would overcome evil.

The world teaches to protect oneself, to love only those that love back, to lend with the expectation to receive. When you became a follower of Jesus, all that changes. Knowing that goodness has the power to overcome evil, love as God loves you. The results will speak for themselves

Day 177

1 Samuel 3:7 Now Samuel did not yet know the Lord, neither was the word of the Lord yet revealed unto him.

Thought: A Commitment To Man Is Different From Knowing God

Focus: How Well Do You Know God?

When young Samuel was brought to Eli, he proved to be a faithful young man. He was obedient to all that Eli requested of him. Though he remained faithful, Samuel did not yet know God. His commitment was to Eli not to God.

Faithfulness and having an obedient spirit are important traits, but they do not necessarily mean that you know God. As you remain faithful to those that have rule over you, insist on knowing God. Position yourself that you are able to hear the voice of the Lord. A commitment to man is different from knowing God.

Day 178

Genesis 3:1 Now the serpent was more subtil than any beast of the field which the Lord God had made.

Thought: Satan Is Out To Destroy You

Focus: Don't Underestimate The Ability Of The Enemy

The Word of God makes it clear; Satan is subtle. He is able to present himself in a manner that seeks to destroy the most committed saint. The greatest weapon against the one that seeks to destroy is obedience to God's Word. Any deviation opens the door to Satan. It is essential that the enemy's ability is not underestimated.

Though you are committed to serving the Lord, you must be aware of the enemy's ability to deceive. He was created as the most subtle animal. No one is exempt from his attacks. His agenda is to kill, steal, and destroy. Stay firm in your knowledge and obedience to God's Word. It is there that you remain safe from his antics. Do not underestimate his ability.

Day 179

Psalm 34:1 I will bless the LORD at all times: his praise shall continually be in my mouth.

Thought: Praise Is Not to Be A Part Time Occurrence

Focus: Is Your Praise Subject To Your Current Situation?

David's life was filled with many challenges, some created by him, others were not. Regardless of the cause or the impact of his struggles, one thing remains constant. David, at all times, had praise for the Lord in his mouth. His praise was not a part time thing.

Your praise for the Lord cannot be limited to the church setting or an occasional event. Your praise is to be a part of your life. Let your praise be such that it invites others to join in with you as you exalt His name. Regardless of what you may be facing, let your soul make a boast in the Lord that others may hear and be glad.

Day 180

Psalm 27:1 The LORD is my light and my salvation; whom shall I fear? the LORD is the strength of my life; of whom shall I be afraid?

Thought: The Lord Is Your Protector; There Is No Need to Be Afraid

Focus: Remain Focused on The Lord; You Need Not Fear

David had many enemies that sought to destroy him. If he had placed his confidence only in himself his life would have been in great turmoil. Understanding his own limitations, he placed his trust in the Lord, declaring he had no need to fear or be afraid. God was the strength of his life.

If your focus is on yourself as others attack you, your life will be filled with fear and doubts. Recognizing that the Lord is your light and your salvation, place your trust in Him. With the Lord as your protector, you will have no need to fear or be afraid.

Day 181

Psalm 25:4-5 Shew me thy ways, O LORD; teach me thy paths. Lead me in thy truth and teach me: for thou art the God of my salvation; on thee do I wait all the day.

Thought: Look To the One That Has Total Truth

Focus: With Patience Wait, He Will Respond

David's complete trust was in his God. It was the Lord that he looked to for his direction and instruction. With assurance, he waited patiently to receive what the Lord had for him. No action was taken until the Lord spoke.

Where one turns for directions is vital. While others may look to a variety of places, with assurance, insist on looking to the Lord. As you wait with patience, you can be assured He will respond. He has what you need for a successful journey.

Day 182

Genesis 22:17-18 That in blessing I will bless thee, and in multiplying I will multiply thy seed as the stars of the heaven, and as the sand which is upon the sea shore; and thy seed shall possess the gate of his enemies; And in thy seed shall all the nations of the earth be blessed; because thou hast obeyed my voice.

Thought: God Honors Obedience

Focus: Faith Opens The Door To Blessings

Abraham's response to the instructions of God demanded great faith. He was told to offer his son Isaac as a burnt offering to the Lord. His faith in God to bless through Isaac, allowed him to be willing to obey. This resulted in him being blessed.

Your faith will be tried by God. The key is, when you hear His voice, obey. As you walk in obedience, you will discover His wonderful blessings flowing into your life. It is a fact, God honors obedience. It will demand faith, but will result in you being blessed.

Day 183

Genesis 22:5 And Abraham said unto his young men, Abide ye hear with the ass; and I and the lad will go yonder and worship, and come again to you.

Thought: Faith Believes The Impossible

Focus: God's Promises Will Be Fulfilled

Abraham had come to a place in his faith that regardless of what appeared, he remained confident that all of God's promises would be fulfilled. When told to offer his son Isaac as a sacrifice, he went forth knowing God's promise would not fail. Whatever it took, the impossible would become possible.

The promises that God has made to you will not fail. As He directs your steps, walk in faith. Circumstances may tell you that your desired results are impossible, but remain confident. God's promises will be fulfilled.

Day 184

Psalm 16:11 Thou wilt shew me the path of life: in thy presence is fulness of joy; At thy right hand there are pleasures for evermore.

Thought: The Lord's Directions Lead To Victory

Focus: Stay In His Presence; Joy Awaits You

David's life was one of trust and dependency on the goodness of the Lord. He was not disappointed. As he placed himself in the presence of the Lord, he found great joy. It was there, that regardless of what he might be facing, he found pleasures for evermore.

In the midst of your challenges, and struggles, do not allow anything to take your joy. Place yourself in the presence of the Lord. It is there you will find joy and pleasure for evermore.

Day 185

Joshua 9:14 And the men took of their victuals and asked not counsel at the mouth of the LORD.

Thought: Before Acting; Ask

Focus: God Knows What You Don't Know

As the people of Israel came into Canaan, they defeated one nation after another. The inhabitants of Gibeon, hearing what had occurred, developed a plan. They came to Joshua, appearing to have come from a long distance, wanting to form a league with them. Joshua, without taking counsel from the Lord, agreed. He mistakenly acted without asking.

The Bible clearly instructs us to acknowledge the Lord in all our ways. When a decision must be made, be prayerful. Before acting, ask the counsel of the Lord. He will direct you in the proper manner. God knows what you don't.

Day 186

Psalm 46:10 Be still and know that I am God: I will be exalted among the heathen, I will be exalted in the earth.

Thought: There Is a Time to Do and A Time To Be Still

Focus: Stay Calm God Is in Charge

No matter what one might face, there is no need to lose hope, nor is it a time to panic and rush into action. Unfortunately, we often rush into doing when we should simply be still. It is essential that before we go forward on our own, we must prayerfully wait on God. He is the one in total control.

Have you ever, in the midst of a challenge, rushed into action, only to regret what you said or did? Learn to wait on God. Before responding to what you are facing, be still. You will soon discover that God is in control of everything.

Day 187

1 Samuel 3:8 And the LORD called Samuel again the third time. And he arose and went to Eli, and said, Here am I; for thou didst call me. And Eli perceived that the LORD had called the child.

Thought: Every Child of God Must Know the Voice of God

Focus: God Has Something to Say to You

As a young child, Samuel was brought to the house of the Lord to be mentored by Eli. Samuel was faithful and obedient to the prophet, but he did not yet know the voice of the Lord. As he grew, the Lord spoke not to Eli but this time to Samuel. The child was confused, but Eli, as a wise leader, instructed Samuel what he was to do. It was essential that Samuel know the voice of God.

Obedience to leadership is vital to the body of Christ. God has placed individuals in place for the training and growth of the saints. This does not mean that God does not speak to His children directly. Position yourself to hear the voice of the Lord. It is essential that you know His voice.

Day 188

1 John 5:14 And this is the confidence that we have in him, that, if we ask any thing according to his will, he heareth us:

Thought: As You Ask According to His Will, Expect to Receive

Focus: God Hears Your Cries

John writes to encourage the believer. He reminds his readers of the importance and blessings that come from walking in the will of God. Those that are, can ask anything, and with confidence expect to receive.

Your walk with God provides you confidence. As you ask, in accordance with His will, you have the right to expect. As you petition Him, be assured that He hears your cries. Your prayers will be answered.

Day 189

Proverbs 15:22 Without counsel purposes are disappointed: but in the multitude of counsellors, they are established.

Thought: Avoid Disappointment, Seek Counsel

Focus: With Counsel Thoughts Can Be Established

Solomon shares with his readers the importance of receiving counsel from others. What may begin as a good idea, without sound advice, will often lead to disappointment. It is with the counsel of others that the same idea can be established.

As the Lord blesses you with thoughts, it is essential that you take advantage of the counsel of others. As Solomon tells us, it is through the multitude of counselors that thoughts are established. Avoid disappointment, seek the advice of others.

Day 190

1 Timothy 4:12 Let no man despise thy youth; but be thou an example of the believers, in word, in conversation, in charity, in spirit, in faith, in purity.

Thought: It Is Not Age; It Is Your Testimony That Matters

Focus: Are You Demonstrating How A Saint Should Live?

Paul's letter to Timothy addressed his youth. The younger man felt the pressure of those that believed that he was too young to lead. Paul counseled him to not allow the attacks to capture his attention. Timothy was told to continue to remain focused on being an example of how a saint should live.

Some may believe you are too young to serve, others feel that you may be too old. Let none of their accusations cause you to lose focus on serving God. Place your attention on being an example to the believer. God will be pleased.

Day 191

Ephesians 4:32 And be ye kind one to another, tenderhearted, forgiving one another, even as God for Christ's sake hath forgiven you.

Thought: As Jesus Was, So Must We Be

Focus: As He Loved Us So We Must Love One Another

Throughout this chapter we are taught the need to be perfected. Each of us has a role to play within the body of Christ. As we seek to fulfill our assignment, love for others must be demonstrated. As Jesus cared for us, we must care one for another.

It matters not what your assignment is, love for others must be present. As Jesus demonstrated his love for us, we must do the same. With a spirit of forgiveness, we must be kind one to another. Let your life show others the fullness of God's love. As Jesus was, so must we be.

Day 192

John 4:28 The woman then left her waterpot, and went her way into the city, and saith to the men.

Thought: Your Past Does Not Need to Keep You From Your Future

Focus: God Has Set You Free to Tell Your Story

The woman at the well heard the gospel message from Jesus. She fully accepted all that she heard and wanted others to know about him. Leaving all behind, she ran into the city and told all to go see about this man. They went because of what they heard, but once they were there and heard the master speak, they believed in themselves.

What occurred before you came to Jesus is not the key. What does matter is what occurs once you hear him. Don't allow your past to keep you from your future; he has set you free. It is time now that your story be heard. Let the world know all that he has to offer.

Day 193

Acts 27:21-22 But after long abstinence Paul stood forth in the midst of them, and said, Sirs, ye should have hearkened unto me, and not have loosed from Crete, and to have gained this harm and loss. And now I exhort you to be of good cheer: for there shall be no loss of any man's life among you, but of the ship.

Thought: In The Midst Of Your Storm, Pray

Focus: It May Not Be Immediately; But God Will Respond

In the midst of a storm that took all hope for the ship that Paul was on, he went before the Lord in prayer. After a long abstinence, Paul declared that an angel of God spoke to him. Though the ship would be destroyed there would be no loss of life. Paul's prayer was heard.

As you face the storms in your life, it is essential that you remain prayerful. Though you do not receive an immediate response, stay before the Lord. Your determination will be honored, your prayer will be heard; God will respond.

Day 194

Proverbs 25:28 He that hath no rule over his own spirit is like a city that is broken down, and without walls.

Thought: Your Spirit Must Be Subject To You

Focus: Every Desire Cannot Be Fulfilled

Within each of us is our "spirit". It is what drives us, it is our personality. The problem is that it does not always seek what is appropriate. It is essential that we control our spirit, realizing that every desire cannot be fulfilled. Victory is obtained as we control our spirit and walk in obedience to the Spirit of the Lord. He will lead you in the proper direction.

Within you are two spirits. The spirit of self and the Spirit of the Lord. The first must be kept under control, while you walk in obedience to the second. Recognizing that every desire cannot be fulfilled, stay in God's presence that you may maintain the proper response to both.

Day 195

Titus 2:7 In all things shewing thyself a pattern of good works: in doctrine shewing uncorruptness, gravity, sincerity, Sound speech, that cannot be condemned; that he that is of the contrary part may be ashamed, having no evil thing to say of you.

Thought: Your Conversation Is Your Greatest Testimony

Focus: Let There Be No Room For Condemnation

Paul's directions to Titus were clear. He was to teach those that sought to follow Christ how to live. Their words and actions should demonstrate a holy and Godly life. There should be no opportunity for the non-believer to speak evil of them. Their conversation is to be their greatest testimony.

How do others see you? Do your actions and words represent a holy God? Is there a consistency in what you say, you believe, and how you conduct your life? Let your words and actions represent who Jesus is. Let there be no room for condemnation.

Day 196

Genesis 32:28 And he said, Thy name shall be called no more Jacob, but Israel: for as a prince hast thou power with God and with men, and hast prevailed.

Thought: God Has A Powerful Future That Awaits You

Focus: Don't Allow Your Past To Keep You From Your Future

Jacob was a supplanter, one that used trickery for his betterment. He could not remain in this state and enjoy the future that God intended for him. It took an all-night wrestling match with God, with Jacob insisting on being blessed. His determination was rewarded. He was no longer Jacob but was now Israel. He now had power with God and man.

The blessings that God has for His children are sometimes blocked because of traits that remain from the past. If you fall into this category, know that God is waiting on you to come before Him with determination. Wrestle if need be, but insist on being blessed. Don't allow your past to keep you from your future. There is much that awaits you

Day 197

Psalm19:1 The heavens declare the glory of God; and the firmament sheweth his handywork.

Thought: The Beauty of God's Creation Reveals Who He Is

Focus: He Who Declared, "Let There Be Light" Can Speak to Your Situation

If you ever travel to what is called the wilderness. It is a peaceful place where one can relax and enjoy the "handiwork of God". It appears illogical to me that so many observe all that is before their eyes and still doubt the existence of God. The beauty of creation did not appear by accident. It was created by the one who declared, "it is very good".

As you take time to both observe and enjoy the Lord's handiwork, let it be a true reminder of His power and authority. The one that placed the sun and the moon into space is able to impact your life. God's creation speaks volumes of who He is.

Day 198

James 1:5 If any of you lack wisdom, let him ask of God, that giveth to all men liberally, and upbraideth not; and it shall be given him.

Thought: There Is No Need To Go Lacking, Ask And Receive

Focus: Wisdom Awaits You

Throughout scripture we read of the importance of wisdom. In Proverbs it is referred to as the principal thing. Where does wisdom come from? James informs us it comes from God. He also shares that it is available to all that ask. There is no need to go lacking, those that ask in faith will receive.

As you go through life, many decisions will be made. You can choose to depend upon your own thoughts or choose rather to obtain Godly wisdom. There is no need to go lacking, ask in faith and receive through your obedience. The Lord awaits your requests, He gives liberally to all that ask in faith while obeying His word.

Day 199

Isaiah 40:31 But they that wait upon the LORD shall renew their strength; they shall mount up with wings as eagles; they shall run, and not be weary; and they shall walk, and not faint.

Thought: The Lord Directs And Provides Strength

Focus: Waiting Pays Off

One's journey in life has many twists and turns, often producing challenges that can be difficult to overcome. Endeavoring to face them without God's help is unwise. Those that are successful are those that have learned how to wait on the Lord. They have learned not to proceed without the Lord's direction and without His strength.

We often react too quickly during challenging times. Our actions tend to make matters worse. As you learn how to wait on the Lord, you will discover that He will both direct you and provide the strength needed for your journey. Waiting pays off.

Day 200

Luke 17:12-14 And as he entered into a certain village, there met him ten men that were lepers, which stood afar off: And they lifted up their voices, and said, Jesus, Master, have mercy on us. And when he saw them, he said unto them, Go shew yourselves unto the priests. And it came to pass, that, as they went, they were cleansed.

Thought: Your Problem Is The Lord's Concern

Focus: As He Directs, Obey, You Will Not Be Disappointed

Ten men stricken with leprosy, forced to call out to the Lord from a distance sought his mercy. Their problem mattered to him. He responded with concern and direction. They went forth in obedience and were healed.

Your problems matter to the Lord. Do not allow despair to set in that you accept defeat. Make your request known unto Him, and then follow His directions. You will not be disappointed.

Day 201

Luke 18:1 And he spake a parable unto them to this end, that men ought always to pray, and not to faint.

Thought: You Need Not Faint; You Can Pray

Focus: Your Victory Is on The Other Side Of Your Prayer

Throughout His earthly ministry, Jesus both taught and demonstrated the importance of prayer. One's prayer life not only brings forth miracles but solidifies one's relationship with God. It is through prayer that we enter the presence of God. It is there that we can receive the comfort of the Lord enabling us to go forth, trusting Him for Godly results. You need not faint; you can pray.

As you pray, you will find your disposition changing. Where doubt was found, faith will now exist. Your confidence will flourish, your prayers will be prayed with expectation as well as with joy. You need not faint, pray. Your victory is on the other side of your prayer.

Day 202

Proverbs 16:7 When a man's ways please the LORD, he maketh even his enemies to be at peace with him.

Thought: The Key Is to Please God

Focus: Don't Allow Anyone to Distract Your Focus

The focus of the saint is critical. As it remains committed to pleasing God, excellent results will occur. He is the one that controls all things including one's enemies. When a man's ways please God, he will make even their enemies to be at peace with him.

How do you respond to your enemies? Has your focus been adjusted to pleasing them more than pleasing God? It is essential that you do not allow anyone to distract your focus. As you please God, He will make all, including your enemies to be at peace with you.

Day 203

Proverbs 15:1 A soft answer turneth away wrath: but grievous words stir up anger.

Thought: Choose Your Words Carefully; They Matter

Focus: You Have the Power to Dilute Strife

The proverb helps us to understand the power of our words. As we choose our words carefully, we can diminish the anger that may exist. If we use the wrong words, we will add to the level that already exists. It is essential that we choose our words carefully.

You have been in conversations that have the potential to result in poor decisions being made because of anger. God has empowered you to diminish that anger. As you choose the proper words, you will be able to turn away from the wrath that is felt. Your words have power.

Day 204

Genesis 50:20 But as for you, ye thought evil against me; but God meant it unto good, to bring to pass, as it is this day, to save much people alive.

Thought: Even The Bad Can Result In Good

Focus: God Is Preparing and Positioning You For Your Future

When we consider the life of Joseph, we see a picture of how bad can result in good. Joseph knew his brothers meant evil but God used their actions for his good. Potiphar's wife, reacting in anger, sought to punish Joseph, but again God used her actions for his good. Each step was a part of Joseph being prepared for his future. Even the bad resulted in good.

As you examine specific incidents in your life, some you will label, "bad". As you continue to look through God's eyes you begin to recognize that the Lord is both preparing, and positioning you, for your future. Though some incidents will cause you to say ouch, there will come a time that you will look back and say thank you. Trust God to order your steps, stay focused on Him and you will not be disappointed. Even the bad will result in good. All things mean all things.

Day 205

Matthew 25:21 His lord said unto him, Well done, thou good and faithful servant: thou hast been faithful over a few things, I will make thee ruler over many things: enter thou into the joy of thy lord.

Thought: Joy Follows Faithfulness

Focus: What God Has Given You Is To Be Used

Jesus shared a parable where talents are given to three different individuals, the first five, the second two, and the third one. The first two used what they were given wisely while the third hid his. Upon the return of the Master, those that added to what they were given were praised and duly rewarded. They would enter a place of joy. The one that hid his talent was rebuked and cast into darkness. What God gives His children; He expects them to use to His glory.

In accordance to your ability, God has equipped you with the ability to bless others and glorify Him. Every child of God has the gifts needed to fulfill their assignment. No one is left out. As you actively use your gift, others will be blessed, and joy will enter your spirit. What the Lord has given you must be used.

Day 206

Proverbs 6:19 A false witness that speaketh lies, and he that soweth discord among brethren.

Thought: God Hates A False Witness And Those That Sow Discord

Focus: Actions Pleasing To God Must Be Maintained

The proverb list six things that God hates. A false witness and those that sow discord are included in this behavior. It is essential, that not only must one not allow such behavior to be demonstrated in their own life, but must be cautious not to allow others to draw them into ungodly responses. Actions pleasing to God must be maintained.

Unfortunately, you will come across those that seek to sow discord among the saints. They do not hesitate to provide a false witness creating additional hostility. This behavior cannot be accepted as proper. We must insist that all of our actions are pleasing to God. A Holy God deserves holy behavior from His children.

Day 207

Proverbs 19:11 The discretion of a man deferreth his anger; and it is his glory to pass over a transgression.

Thought: Every Offense Does Not Need Your Attention

Focus: A Discreet Person Knows What Not To See

Offenses are a part of everyday life. Where some may need attention, discretion teaches us that most do not require any action. Wisdom allows one to distinguish between those that do require a response and those that do not. A discreet person knows what not to see.

A person that practices discretion does not respond to every offense. He knows what not to see, realizing any action taken would simply make matters worse. As you learn what not to see, your life will flow much smoother.

Day 208

Matthew 14:36 And besought him that they might only touch the hem of his garment: and as many as touched were made perfectly whole.

Thought: His Blessings Are Not Limited to One

Focus: He Awaits All That He Might Bless

We often are told about the woman with the issue of blood, who touched the hem of his garment, and was healed. It is a powerful story of one person's faith, but she was not the only one to be blessed in this manner. As many that came to touch him, as she did, were also made whole. God's blessings are not limited to just one. He awaits all that he might bless.

As you hear of how others were blessed by God, let it be an encouragement to you. As others have been blessed so may you be also. His blessings are not limited to one or two. Go before Him, in faith, knowing that He can bless all that seek Him.

Day 209

1 Peter 2:1-2 Wherefore laying aside all malice, and all guile, and hypocrisies, and envies, and all evil speakings, As newborn babes, desire the sincere milk of the word, that ye may grow thereby.

Thought: A New You Is Being Formed

Focus: The Old Shall Be Replaced With The New

As Peter addresses the believer, he reminds them of the changes that are now expected in their lives. Malice, hypocrisy, and evil speaking can no longer be a part of who they are. They must all be laid aside, as they grow through their desire for God's Word. A new person is being formed.

As you entered the Kingdom of God, you brought who you were with you. Through your desire for God's Word, growth will take place. You will lay aside those things that do not represent God or who you now are. You are becoming the new person God called you to be.

Day 210

Ephesians 4:28 Let him that stole steal no more: but rather let him labour, working with his hands the thing which is good, that he may have to give to him that needeth.

Thought: Total Change Is Your Goal

Focus: Victory Can Be Measured In Behavior

Paul makes it clear that there are areas in the life of the saint that require total change. Certainly to cease from stealing deserves celebration, but it is not the complete goal. Total change moves one from being a taker to becoming a giver. It is not simply heard in one's words, but true change is measured in behavior.

How far have you traveled in your journey to change? How do you compare to Paul's example? In this verse, the one that stole is not only to stop stealing, but now to work with his hands that he might have to give to those in need. Let your life demonstrate complete change.

Day 211

Matthew 9:18 While he spake these things unto them, behold, there came a certain ruler, and worshipped him, saying, My daughter is even now dead: but come and lay thy hand upon her, and she shall live.

Thought: Pray With Expectation

Focus: Why Ask If You Don't Believe?

A father, whose daughter was near death, came to Jesus seeking his help. He beseeched the Master, asking him to come lay his hand upon the child. His request was made with expectation, declaring if he did his daughter would live.

Prayer is an integral part of a saint's life. While some simply go through the motions, others anticipate a positive response. As you pray, do so with expectation, knowing God honors faith. There is no need to ask if you do not believe.

Day 212

Psalm 119:28 My soul melteth for heaviness: strengthen thou me according unto thy word.

Thought for the Day: When Heaviness Attacks His Word Provides Strength

Reflection for the Day: God's Word Provides Stability

In the lives of all, there are times when heaviness attacks. When this occurs the remedy is to turn to God's Word. It is there that strength is provided. Amid confusion, the Word provides stability.

You, as well as others, will find yourself in the midst of heaviness. It is essential that you do not allow it to overwhelm you. Turn to the Word of God. It will provide the strength and stability needed to go forward in the Lord.

Day 213

Psalm19:1 The heavens declare the glory of God; and the firmament sheweth his handywork.

Thought: The Beauty Of God's Creation Reveals Who He Is.

Focus: He Who Declared, "Let There Be Light" Can Speak To Your Situation

This November, I travel to what I call the wilderness. It is said to be a peaceful place where one can relax and enjoy the "handywork of God." It appears illogical to me that so many may observe all that is before their eyes and still doubt the existence of God. The beauty of creation did not appear by accident. It was created by the one who declared, "it is very good."

As you take time to both observe and enjoy the Lord's handywork, let it be a true reminder of His power and authority. The one that placed the sun and the moon into space is able to impact your life. God's creation speaks volumes of who He is.

Day 214

Galatians 5:16-17 This I say then, Walk in the Spirit, and ye shall not fulfil the lust of the flesh. For the flesh lusteth against the Spirit, and the Spirit against the flesh: and these are contrary the one to the other: so that ye cannot do the things that ye would.

Thought: The Battle Remains; Walk In The Spirit

Focus: Your Flesh Must Be Denied

Within each of us, a battle takes place. The Spirit seeks to lead us in the will of God, while our flesh seeks to please itself. They are contrary one to another. We must learn to deny our flesh and walk in the Spirit. It is in the Spirit that we have victory.

As the Spirit seeks to guide you, your flesh will cry out to be pleased. Knowing that the Spirit offers you victory, your flesh must be denied. Do not allow flesh to cause you to compromise. It is in God that you will have peace.

Day 215

Proverb 19:20 Hear counsel and receive instruction, that thou mayest be wise in thy latter end.

Thought: What You Learn Today Will Bless You Tomorrow

Focus: Have An Ear to Receive Sound Instruction

The Lord is constantly preparing us for tomorrow. He provides, through others, counsel, and instruction so that we may gain wisdom. It is essential that we have an ear to receive sound instruction. It is there today to prepare us for our tomorrow.

You are being prepared for your future. The Lord has placed men and women into your life that will provide sound counsel and instruction. With gladness, let them pour into your life. Apply what they provide so that you might be prepared for your tomorrow.

Day 216

Psalm 32:5 I acknowledged my sin unto thee, and mine iniquity have I not hid. I said, I will confess my transgressions unto the LORD; and thou forgavest the iniquity of my sin. Selah.

Thought: Repentance Begins with Acknowledgement

Focus: Repentance Results in Forgiveness

David shares in this Psalm what he endured when he remained silent before God after committing adultery. It was a time of great discomfort. All that changed when he acknowledged his sin and repented before his God. It was then that he knew he was forgiven. Repentance began with his acknowledgment.

Forgiveness of sin is a gift that God has made available to all His children. The process begins with the acknowledgment of the sin, accompanied with the sorrow of realizing that you have offended God with your behavior. It is through this process that forgiveness of sin is experienced. Silence is not the answer, acknowledgment is the initial step.

Day 217

1 Thessalonians 4:9 But as touching brotherly love ye need not that I write unto you: for ye yourselves are taught of God to love one another.

Thought: Instruction Comes First From God

Focus: Your Obedience Will Bless You And Others

God has placed into his church teachers to instruct us in the ways of the Lord. There are certain areas that our instruction comes directly from God. The Holy Ghost teaches that we must love one another. Our obedience is mandatory.

God has provided you, His Spirit. As He instructs you, it is mandatory that you respond in obedience. His teaching begins with His commandment to love another. Your obedience will bless both you and others.

Day 218

1 Thessalonians 5:21 Prove all things; hold fast that which is good.

Thought: Prayerful Consideration Is Needed in All Areas

Focus: Hold On to What Is Of God, Let Go Of What Is Not

Paul, in his teaching to the saints at Thessalonica, cautions them not to rush into coming to final decisions. Many ideas and concepts will be presented to them. As they are, prayerful consideration is needed. They are to prove all things. That which is of God must be held onto, the rest is to be let go.

When presented with ideas and biblical interpretations, do not be in a rush to quickly accept or reject. It is needful to prove all things. Prayerfully give thought to what is of God and what is not. Hold on to what is, while letting go of what is not.

Day 219

John 4:9 Then saith the woman of Samaria unto him, How is it that thou, being a Jew, askest drink of me, which am a woman of Samaria? for the Jews have no dealings with the Samaritans.

Thought: No One Is Exempt from God's Love

Focus: Christ Died for All Mankind

The chapter begins by telling us that it was essential that Jesus go through Samaria. Though, Jews typically went around Samaria, there was a woman there that needed to know who Jesus was. Jesus ignored that Jews despised Samaritans and considered women to be inferior. No one lived outside his love. He died for all mankind.

Unfortunately, there is often decisions made as to who we share the gospel with. We place limits on who we believe would receive the gospel message. It is essential that we understand that no one is outside God's love. Christ died for all mankind.

Day 220

John 3:16 For God so loved the world, that he gave his only begotten Son, that whosoever believeth in him should not perish, but have everlasting life.

Thought: Love Has A Cost

Focus: He Sacrificed Because He Loves Us

As we read this familiar scripture, we note the sacrifice God made that we might obtain salvation. His love resulted in the giving of his only begotten son. Love has a cost.

We constantly hear about the love we have one for another. While it is easy to make that statement, it must not be forgotten that love has a cost. As you speak of your love for others, be prepared to make the sacrifice that is required to meet their need. Love has a cost.

Day 221

1 Timothy 4:16 Take heed unto thyself, and unto the doctrine; continue in them: for in doing this thou shalt both save thyself, and them that hear thee.

Thought: Stay Focused on Truth; Good Results Will Follow

Focus: You Have the Power to Bless Others

Paul's instructions to Timothy highlight the importance of staying focused on walking in truth. He reminds the younger man, as his life demonstrates the truth of God's Word, not only will he be blessed, but will also be providing an opportunity for others to follow.

Your choices not only have an impact on your life but also on others. As you stay focused on walking in truth, you are giving others the opportunity to follow. You, through your commitment, could bless not only yourself, but also others.

Day 222

2 Chronicles 14:11 And Asa cried unto the LORD his God, and said, LORD, it is nothing with thee to help, whether with many, or with them that have no power: help us, O LORD our God; for we rest on thee, and in thy name we go against this multitude. O LORD, thou art our God; let not man prevail against thee.

Thought: Numbers Matter Not To The Lord

Focus: Your Enemy Is No Match For God

Asa, King of Judah, placed his trust in the Lord. Though Judah had a well-equipped army they were greatly outmanned by the Ethiopians. Asa was not impacted by the size of the enemy; his trust was in his God. He knew the number did not impact the Lord. God slew the Ethiopians, as they fled before Judah.

The size of your enemy matters not to the Lord. He is not impacted by anyone or anything. As you place your trust in Him you will not be disappointed. Your enemy is no match for the Lord.

Day 223

Luke 11:1 And it came to pass, that, as he was praying in a certain place, when he ceased, one of his disciples said unto him, Lord, teach us to pray, as John also taught his disciples.

Thought: Without Prayer There Is No Fellowship, Without Fellowship There Is No True Relationship

Focus: If You Don't Learn Anything Else, Learn How to Pray

As the disciples of the Lord observed the Lord's prayer life and the results that followed, they wisely asked the Master to teach them to pray. They soon discovered that it was through the fellowship of prayer that their relationship with Him developed. It was prayer that they needed to learn.

You have heard that it is your relationship with the Lord that matters. This is true but it is also true that without fellowship there can be no true relationship. Follow the wisdom of the disciples and ask the Lord to teach you how to pray. If you don't learn anything else, learn to pray. The rest will follow.

Day 224

Mark 14:38 Watch ye and pray, lest ye enter into temptation. The spirit truly is ready, but the flesh is weak.

Thought: There Is a Battle That Must Be Fought

Focus: The Victory Is in The Prayer

Knowing that the soldiers were soon to come, Jesus went to the Garden of Gethsemane to pray. He took all his disciples with him but only brought Peter, James, and John into the Garden with him. It was time to gain victory over self, one that would come only through intense prayer. Jesus endeavored to help the three understand that though one's spirit may be willing, flesh remains weak. It was a lesson that they learned through failure. The disciples slept while Jesus prayed. His battle was won, theirs was not.

In each of our lives, as we travel with the Lord, we will face challenges that demand fervent prayer. The struggle will be to deny accepting what our flesh wants. It is a victory that will come only through prayer. Find your Garden of Gethsemane and remain there until it is no longer your will that matters, but the will of the Father. It is in your prayer that victory will be discovered.

Day 225

Numbers 14:5 Then Moses and Aaron fell on their faces before all the assembly of the congregation of the children of Israel.

Thought: In The Midst of Opposition; Pray

Focus: Your Victory Is in God's Hands

After hearing the negative report brought from ten of the spies that were sent to see Canaan, the Israelites were ready to choose a captain and return to Egypt. Uncertain as to how to respond, Moses and Aaron fell on their faces before the Lord. In the midst of their opposition, they turned to the one who held their victory in His hands.

When one faces opposition, how they respond is key. While some panic, others jump too quickly into action. When you find yourself under attack do neither. Fall on your face before the Lord and place all into His hands. He has everything under control. Your victory is in His hands.

Day 226

Acts 10:25-26 And as Peter was coming in, Cornelius met him, and fell down at his feet, and worshipped him. But Peter took him up, saying, Stand up; I myself also am a man.

Thought: It Is God Not Man Who Has The Power

Focus: You May Honor A Man But Only God Is To Be Worshipped

God spoke to both Peter and Cornelius. He instructed Cornelius to send for the man of God while at the same time sending Peter to carry the gospel message to Cornelius. As Peter entered, Cornelius fell at his feet and began to worship the Apostle. Peter quickly told him rise, stating clearly he was only a man. You may honor a man but only God is to be worshipped.

Within the church culture, we are taught properly to show honor one to another. It is appropriate to show respect to those who lead us but our respect cannot be allowed to move to worship. Only God is to be worshipped. The power comes from God, not from man. He alone is to be worshipped.

Day 227

Matthew 3:1-2 In those days came John the Baptist, preaching in the wilderness of Judaea, And saying, Repent ye: for the kingdom of heaven is at hand.

Thought: Every Journey Has A Starting Point

Focus: Your Walk With God Must Begin With Repentance

One cannot look at the life of Jesus without giving thought to John the Baptist, the voice crying in the wilderness. John's message was clear, to walk with Jesus, one first had to repent. The journey with the Lord could begin only with a changed life.

Regardless of how much one can quote scripture or be active in a local congregation, the journey with the Lord must begin with repentance. Take a prayerful look at your life, with a mind to please God. Your journey with the Lord will be a blessed one but it must begin with, and continue with, a repentant spirit.

Day 228

Ezra 10:1 Now when Ezra had prayed, and when he had confessed, weeping and casting himself down before the house of God, there assembled unto him out of Israel a very great congregation of men and women and children: for the people wept very sore.

Thought: Your Prayer Has The Power To Change Others

Focus: Pray With Fervency And Determination

God's people had sinned, they left the will of God. Ezra, being extremely distressed over their actions, was driven to prayer. His prayer was one of fervency and determination. It had an impact; those that had offended the Word repented and corrected their actions. Ezra's prayer changed the actions of others.

What influence can you have on those that will not listen to your words? Though you may feel you have no power, you do. Go fervently before the Lord in prayer. With confidence, cry out before Him knowing that He will hear your petition. Your prayer has the power to change lives.

Day 229

Matthew 6:24 No man can serve two masters: for either he will hate the one, and love the other; or else he will hold to the one, and despise the other. Ye cannot serve God and mammon.

Thought: God Or Riches; A Choice Must Be Made

Focus: No One Can Serve Two Masters

The scriptures teach us that where your treasure is your heart will be also. Choices in life are essential in all areas, especially in determining what is most important to us. Though it is true God has the ability to bless His children greatly, riches must not be the focal point of one's heart. The love for the Lord cannot have competition with anything; a choice must be made.

As you take a careful look at what drives you, are you driven to please God or are riches what determines your decision? It is essential that you understand that there can only be one master in your life. A choice must be made as to who you will serve. Be assured that if you choose the Lord that He will meet all of your needs. He is the proper and wise choice.

Day 230

1 Corinthians 15:33 Be not deceived: evil communications corrupt good manners.

Thought: Choose Your Friends Wisely

Focus: Those You Spend Time With Will Impact Your Behavior

George Washington, our first president, shared an essential biblical principle. He stated, "Associate yourself with people of good quality, for it is better to be alone than in bad company". He understood the impact others had on you. As Paul stated in scripture, we must carefully choose who we spend time with. It is important that we understand the impact they will have on our lives. We must choose those that add value and avoid those that corrupt.

Believing that those that you spend time with, do not impact your behavior, is to deceive yourself. While you must show yourself friendly to all, choose wisely those you bring closest to you. Their behavior will impact yours. Seek to add value to others while not allowing them to affect you.

Day 231

John 13:14 If I then, your Lord and Master, have washed your feet; ye also ought to wash one another's feet.

Thought: The Example Has Been Set

Focus: As Jesus Served Others So Must We Serve

As the time for his departure drew nigh, Jesus demonstrated to his disciples the importance of servanthood. As he washed their feet, they too must be prepared to serve others. They were called to be servants.

Servanthood is a necessary part of one's calling. No matter what title you have or office you might hold, you have been called to serve. Jesus has set the example for all of us to follow. As he served, we must also serve.

Day 232

John 11:4 When Jesus heard that, he said, This sickness is not unto death, but for the glory of God, that the Son of God might be glorified thereby.

Thought: Your Challenge Is Meant For Good

Focus: God Is Aware Of Your Situation

When word was sent to Jesus, informing him of the seriousness of the sickness of his friend Lazarus, Jesus responded that the sickness was not unto death, but to reveal the glory of God. He was aware of the situation.

There are challenges that you will face that may cause you to be quite concerned. Be aware that the Lord is aware of all that you encounter. Many of which are there not to hinder, but to reveal His glory.

Day 233

2 Timothy 2:24-25 And the servant of the Lord must not strive; but be gentle unto all men, apt to teach, patient, In meekness instructing those that oppose themselves; if God peradventure will give them repentance to the acknowledging of the truth.

Thought: Teach Don't Attack

Focus: Provide Truth, Trust God To Bring To Repentance

An attacking spirit does not reflect the Lord nor does it tend to be successful. A child of God should possess a meek spirit, one that teaches even those that oppose themselves. The Lord would have His followers present the Word with gentleness, while trusting God to bring repentance.

Your desire to bring others to repentance is best served with a gentle spirit. With meekness, share God's Word with all, even with those that oppose themselves. As you share, recognize that your trust is in the Lord. He is the one that will bring all to repentance.

Day 234

John 11:22 But I know, that even now, whatsoever thou wilt ask of God, God will give it thee.

Thought: It Is Never Too Late for God to Bless

Focus: It Is Not Time to Give Up

Two sisters were confused and hurt. When their brother Lazarus became sick, they sent for Jesus. They knew that he would come, and their brother would be well. Though he had gotten the word of Lazarus's condition, Jesus delayed his coming. By the time he arrived Lazarus had been dead for four days and placed in his tomb. When Jesus arrived, Martha shared her disappointment with him but added, even now whatsoever you ask of the Father he will give it thee. It is never too late for God to bless.

In each of our lives there are dreams that appear to be lost forever. All logic points to the fact that they are simply memories of prayers that will not be fulfilled. When those feelings of doubt attack remind yourself, God is not limited to anything. It is never too late for Him to bless. It is not the time to give up.

Day 235

Luke 8:48 And he said unto her, Daughter, be of good comfort: thy faith hath made thee whole; go in peace.

Thought: Your Faith Has the Power to Change Any Situation

Focus: As The Spirit Speaks; Obey

Twelve years, a woman with an issue of blood suffered. Though she physically grew weaker, when she heard about Jesus her faith elevated. Her faith drove her beyond what appeared possible. She had to touch the hem of his garment. In obedience to the spirit, she pressed her way through the crowd. There she touched the Master and was made whole.

Faith must be put to work. It demands obedience to the Spirit. It is when one walks in compliance with the directions of the Spirit that miracles occur. Your faith has the power to change anything. Obey and be blessed.

Day 236

Psalm 133:1 Behold, how good and how pleasant it is for brethren to dwell together in unity!

Thought: Where There Is Unity, You Will Find Joy

Focus: Seek To Walk in Unity; Good Things Will Occur

David speaks, in this psalm, of the impact of God's children working in unity. Both a pleasant spirit and excellent results will take place when this occurs. It is essential that each of us makes a determined effort to walk in unity with all.

Though you cannot control the actions of others, you are responsible to seek to work in unity with all. As you set the tone, prayerfully others will follow. This will result in both a pleasant spirit and positive results.

Day 237

Genesis 1:3 And God said, Let there be light: and there was light.

Thought: When God Speaks; Things Take Place

Focus: He Has the Power to Create

In the beginning of time, God spoke, and creation took place. During darkness, He spoke, and light appeared. Over the recorded days of creation, the Lord spoke and all that He declared took place. He is the creator.

Though all that God chose to create has been put into place, God's power has not diminished. When He speaks things take place. He can speak to any situation you currently face and bring deliverance. All power is in His hand.

Day 238

Psalm 34:19 Many are the afflictions of the righteous: but the LORD delivereth him out of them all.

Thought: Today's Struggle Will Be Tomorrow's Testimony

Focus: The Lord Is Your Deliverer

Afflictions arise in the lives of all who seek to follow God. The joy comes from knowing that whatever one might face, deliverance is coming. What you are facing today will be tomorrow's testimony. The Lord is your deliverer.

As you face your struggles, there is no need to lose hope. You have a God that has the power to deliver you, no matter what you face. Today's affliction is simply tomorrow's testimony. The Lord is your deliverer.

Day 239

Hebrews 6:15 And so, after he had patiently endured, he obtained the promise.

Thought: Wait Patiently, You Will Not Be Disappointed

Focus: God's Timing Is Not Man's

God made a promise to Abraham, he would bless him and multiply him. The promise was fulfilled, but not before many years passed filled with many challenges. Throughout all those years, Abraham continued to look to the Lord. His faith was not diminished nor without reward. After he patiently endured, he received the promise.

Every promise God makes will be fulfilled. What must be understood is that the Lord's timing is different than man's timing. With patience, endure all that is before you. As you continue to grow, while you wait, your walk with God will become closer. Stay focused on Him, you will not be disappointed.

Day 240

1 Peter 4:12-13 Beloved, think it not strange concerning the fiery trial which is to try you, as though some strange thing happened unto you: But rejoice, inasmuch as ye are partakers of Christ's sufferings; that, when his glory shall be revealed, ye may be glad also with exceeding joy.

Thought: Don't Be Shocked; Trials Will Come

Focus: Greater Joy Follows The Suffering

It is not uncommon for those that walk with the Lord to focus only on our time on earth. They place no focus on what follows. Yes, there will be suffering here, but a greater joy awaits us. As we move from this world to eternity, a greater joy awaits us.

Your walk with God will include suffering. As you face these challenging times, you must stay focused on what comes next. In the same way that you will suffer with Christ, you will reign with him. A greater joy awaits you.

Day 241

1 Timothy 6:11 But thou, O man of God, flee these things; and follow after righteousness, godliness, faith, love, patience, meekness.

Thought: Knowing What to Flee and What To Seek Is Essential

Focus: It Is in God That Your Blessings Await You

As Paul shares with Timothy, he charges him to flee earthly riches and turn his attention to his walk with the Lord. While others seek the things of this world, his attention must be on godliness, righteousness, faith, love, patience, and meekness. It is in these things that he will find the blessings that await him.

What has your attention? Do you spend your time focused on the riches of this world, or are you seeking a closer walk with God? While the former will entangle you, it is in the will of God that your blessings await you. It is essential that you know what to flee and what to seek.

Day 242

Proverb 3:6 In all thy ways acknowledge him, and he shall direct thy paths.

Thought: God Is Waiting to Direct Your Steps

Focus: Acknowledge Him, Directions Will Follow

Unfortunately, we too often go forth on our own. We do not take time to acknowledge the Lord and receive His directions. This is unwise. As we are instructed, if we acknowledge Him in all our ways, He will direct our steps. He is waiting to be acknowledged.

As you look back at your life, how often did you go forth on your own, only to regret your decision. As you go forward, take time in all your ways, and acknowledge Him. God will direct your steps in a manner that you will be grateful. God is waiting to hear from you.

Day 243

Joshua 1:9 Have not I commanded thee? Be strong and of a good courage; be not afraid, neither be thou dismayed: for the LORD thy God is with thee whithersoever thou goest.

Thought: There Is No Need to Be Afraid; God Is With You

Focus: He Is Your Strength

Joshua, after the death of Moses, was fearful regarding his ability to lead. Those nations that opposed Israel had caused him great anxiety. Amid his doubts, God spoke to him, "have I not commanded you, be strong and of good courage". The Lord wanted Joshua to understand that there was no need to be afraid, God was his strength.

As you follow the directions of the Lord, there will be times when your human emotions will respond to the challenges that you face. At those times, it is essential that you remind yourself that God is with you. There is no need to be afraid.

Day 244

Joshua 4:6-7 That this may be a sign among you, that when your children ask their fathers in time to come, saying, What mean ye by these stones? Then ye shall answer them, That the waters of Jordan were cut off before the ark of the covenant of the LORD; when it passed over Jordan, the waters of Jordan were cut off: and these stones shall be for a memorial unto the children of Israel forever.

Thought: The Story Must Be Told

Focus: We Must Never Forget How God Brought Us Through

After all of the people of Israel crossed over on dry land, the Lord had Joshua to send twelve men, one from each tribe, to carry a rock from where they had crossed. The rocks were placed as a memorial of what God had done. When their children would see the rocks, and ask why they were there, they would tell them what God had done. They were to never forget how God brought them across.

There have been many times in your life when God has miraculously brought you through. These times must never be forgotten. Not only must you know what He did, but others must also hear the story. Your story must be told.

Day 245

Joshua 5:12 And the manna ceased on the morrow after they had eaten of the old corn of the land; neither had the children of Israel manna any more; but they did eat of the fruit of the land of Canaan that year.

Thought: Your Season Is About To Change

Focus: You Have Been Prepared For This Day

For forty years, God led Israel through the wilderness. While the older generation was dying off, a younger one was being taught to trust God. They were being prepared to walk in faith. No longer would they eat manna, they would now eat the fruit of the new land. Their season had changed.

Your life is a journey. There are numerous seasons you will face as you walk with the Lord. Each one prepares you for the next, all leading you to the place of promise. Your season is about to change. You are about to enter your place of promise.

Day 246

Luke 5:16 And he withdrew himself into the wilderness, and prayed.

Thought: It Is Through Prayer That One's Strength Is Replenished

Focus: Spiritual Fatigue Must Not Be Ignored

As the fame of Jesus continued to grow, multitudes sought him out seeking to be healed. Jesus responded to their needs, but then withdrew himself into the wilderness to pray. It was through prayer that his strength was replenished.

As you commit yourself to the work of the Lord, you will face not only physical fatigue but also spiritual fatigue. It is essential that you establish a quiet place where you can pray. It is there that your strength will be replenished.

Day 247

Luke 5:12-13 And it came to pass, when he was in a certain city, behold a man full of leprosy: who seeing Jesus fell on his face, and besought him, saying, Lord, if thou wilt, thou canst make me clean. And he put forth his hand, and touched him, saying, I will: be thou clean. And immediately the leprosy departed from him.

Thought: Come Before God With Expectation

Focus: Your Faith Will Be Honored

As Jesus traveled in a certain city, he was approached by a man stricken with leprosy. The man fell on his face declaring that Jesus was able to make him whole. Jesus responded to his faith, touched his hand, and the man was cleansed. His faith was honored.

Faith is a powerful weapon. As you learn to come before the Lord, with expectation, you will discover your faith will be honored. Approach the Master, knowing He has the power to change your situation.

Day 248

Luke 5:6-7 And when they had this done, they inclosed a great multitude of fishes: and their net brake. And they beckoned unto their partners, which were in the other ship, that they should come and help them. And they came, and filled both the ships, so that they began to sink.

Thought: The Work Is Too Great for One

Focus: We Are Workers Together

As Peter and the other fishermen responded to the command of Jesus, their nets became overfilled with fish. Recognizing what was occurring, they called for their partners to help. They soon learned that the work was too great for one. They were workers together.

The experiences that Jesus leads you through, each has a needful lesson for you. One such lesson is the importance of working together. The work that lies before you is too great for one. You will discover that when you work together greater results will come. We are workers together.

Day 249

Luke 5:4 Now when he had left speaking, he said unto Simon, Launch out into the deep, and let down your nets for a draught.

Thought: There Are Greater Works That Await You

Focus: It Will Require The Enlargement Of Your Faith

Peter and the other fishermen had toiled all night with no success. When Jesus commanded them to go back out, they questioned him, but at his word obeyed. Their obedience was not without results. There was now a greater understanding of who he was. They were being enlarged.

As you continue your walk with the Lord, be aware that He is continually seeking to enlarge you. Your faith will be tested. As it is, respond in obedience, greater works await you.

Day 250

Matthew 12:36 But I say unto you, That every idle word that men shall speak, they shall give account thereof in the day of judgment.

Thought: Give Thought Before You Speak

Focus: What Does Not Add Value Need Not Be Spoken

As Jesus taught, he spoke of the heart being the source of our words. As the heart is evil, what is spoken will be evil. The good heart will speak that which is good. He added to this the importance of avoiding idle words. What does not add value, need not be spoken. Thought should be given before we speak.

Your words have power. They will have impact on the listener. As you seek to add value to others, give thought to what you are about to say. If they will not have a positive result, they need not be spoken. There is no need for idle words.

Day 251

Psalm 27:1 The Lord is my light and my salvation; whom shall I fear? The Lord is the strength of my life; of whom shall I be afraid?

Thought: Those That Walk with The Lord Have No Need To Fear

Focus: His Strength Will See You Through

David understood what it was to face enemies. Throughout his life he faced constant attacks. In the midst of all that he encountered, he declared there was no need to fear. He was not dependent on his own strength but had the joy of knowing the Lord was his strength. There was no need to fear or be afraid.

You will face various attacks and will face those that oppose you. Regardless of their might you need not fear. Your confidence is not in self but rather in knowing that the Lord is your strength. With joy, go forth knowing that you are coming out victorious.

Day 252

Psalm 20:7 Some trust in chariots, and some in horses: but we will remember the name of the Lord our God.

Thought: Regardless Of the Need; God Has Your Name

Focus: Stay Focused on The One That Has Your Help

Throughout the history of Israel, they repetitively forgot God and turned to others for assistance. Each time they made that decision they soon discovered it was the wrong choice. They needed to stay focused on God. He alone was the one that could deliver.

During times of distress, you may be tempted to seek help from a source rather than God. That would be a mistake. Never allow your mind to drift elsewhere. He alone has the power and the compassion to bring deliverance to your situation. Others may call on horses and chariots, stay focused and call upon the Lord.

Day 253

Psalm 46:1 God is our refuge and strength, a very present help in trouble.

Thought: Don't Panic; Your Help Is Present

Focus: In The Midst of Trouble; You Have A Place Of Refuge

Trouble comes to each of us. The key is how one responds to those challenging times. The psalmist informs us that there is no need to panic; our help is present. The Lord not only is a deliverer, but in the midst of the challenge provides us with strength and comfort. He is our refuge.

When trouble comes against you how do you respond? Without a developed relationship with the Lord, panic may be your response. As a mature saint you need not panic. Your help is present; rejoice as you watch God work.

Day 254

Exodus 2:3 And when she could not longer hide him, she took for him an ark of bulrushes, and daubed it with slime and with pitch, and put the child therein; and she laid it in the flags by the river's brink.

Thought: Faith Is Not Always Waiting; It May Demand Action

Focus: You Are A Part Of The Plan

Knowing that her newborn son was to be sacrificed, Jochebed, with boldness and creativity, developed a plan to save him. After hiding the child for three months, she built a small "ark" for him and placed him into the water. Miriam, the infant's older sister, was sent to observe what would happen. By the providence of God, the daughter of Pharaoh was there to take the child to safety. God's plan was fulfilled.

You are a part of God's plan. There will be times you will be called upon to act in boldness, with creativity. Your actions will be coupled with the providence of God resulting in God's will being accomplished.

Day 255

Luke 22:40 And when he was at the place, he said unto them, Pray that ye enter not into temptation.

Thought: A Consistent Prayer Life Prepares You For Tomorrow's Challenges

Focus: Do You Pray Before Or After The Attack

Temptation comes to everyone. Jesus, understanding that concept, endeavored to teach his disciples the necessity of prayer. Not only did he enter the garden to pray, but he brought Peter, James, and John with him. He made it clear to them the purpose of their prayer, pray that you fall not into temptation. The prayer was to be prayed before not after the challenge came.

How consistent is your prayer life? Is it consistent enough that you hear the voice of God warning you of what lies before you? Is it consistent enough to prepare you to face any challenge that might come? If you pray today, you will be ready for tomorrow's challenge. Now is the time to pray.

Day 256

Proverbs 1:7 The fear of the LORD is the beginning of knowledge: but fools despise wisdom and instruction.

Thought: Your Fear Of The Lord Opens The Door To Knowledge

Focus: Wisdom Awaits You

The proverb helps us to understand the necessity of one's acknowledgment and respect for an all knowing God. The fear of the Lord opens one's spirit to be taught the things of God. It is the fool that refuses to be taught. They despise wisdom and instruction.

Your respect for God has opened the door that you may gain wisdom and knowledge. Your awareness that His teachings will bless has opened the door for you to receive all that He has for you. It began with your acknowledgment and respect for who God is.

Day 257

Matthew 20:31 And the multitude rebuked them, because they should hold their peace: but they cried the more, saying, Have mercy on us, O Lord, thou Son of David.

Thought: Others May Say No; But God Will Say Yes

Focus: Your Faith Will Be Rewarded

Two blind men, as Jesus passed by, cried out asking for his mercy. As the multitude sought to quiet them, they cried even the more. Jesus hearing their cry, asked them what they were seeking. He responded to their request by touching their eyes restoring their sight. Their faith was rewarded.

God can place a prayer into a person's spirit that others believe cannot be realized. It is key that the doubts of others are not allowed to destroy the faith of the individual. If God has shown you His desire to bless, let no one stop your prayer. Your faith will be rewarded.

Day 258

Acts 12:15 And they said unto her, Thou art mad. But she constantly affirmed that it was even so. Then said they, It is his angel.

Thought: What You Know You Know

Focus: Do Not Allow The Doubts Of Others To Destroy Your Faith

Herod had Peter placed in prison, with the intent to have him killed after the Passover. The church sought God on behalf of Peter. They prayed without ceasing. God honored their cries and sent an angel to set Peter free. When Peter came to where they were praying, Rhoda heard Peter's voice. She quickly told all those that had been in prayer what she heard. They told her it was not possible, she was mad. She did not allow their doubts to cause her to now doubt. She knew what she knew.

As God responds to your prayers, others may doubt what God has revealed to you. It is essential that you do not allow the doubts of others to cause you to doubt. What you know cannot be influenced by the lack of faith of others. What you know, you know.

Day 259

Acts 9:15 But the Lord said unto him, Go thy way: for he is a chosen vessel unto me, to bear my name before the Gentiles, and kings, and the children of Israel.

Thought: God Chooses Whomever He Desires

Focus: Your Past Need Not Keep You From Your Future

Saul, believing the teachings of the church were false, sought to stop their work. As he was seeking to bring all that he could to the High Priest, the Lord revealed himself to him as the Christ. To the surprise of all, the man who fought the church, was now being called by God to carry His Word. His past did not keep him from his future.

All of us have a past, for many it was a life lived in opposition to the ways of God. No matter what your past was, be assured that God chooses whom He desires. Your past need not keep you from your future.

Day 260

Acts 6:3 Wherefore, brethren, look ye out among you seven men of honest report, full of the Holy Ghost and wisdom, whom we may appoint over this business.

Thought: A Godly Work Requires A Godly Person

Focus: Wisdom, Honesty, And The Holy Spirit Are Essential

As the church grew, there was a need for others to share in the ministry. The apostles instructed the brethren to select seven men to assist in the serving of the widows. Those that they selected must be Godly men. They must be honest, full of the Holy Ghost and wisdom. A Godly work requires Godly people.

Within the organizational church, we often find individuals wanting to serve. Their desire may be good, but there is a criteria God requires. Wisdom, honesty, and a life led by the Holy Spirit are essential. It takes a Godly person to properly do a Godly job.

Day 261

Acts 4:24 And when they heard that, they lifted up their voice to God with one accord, and said, Lord, thou art God, which hast made heaven, and earth, and the sea, and all that in them is:

Thought: When Opposition Comes; Pray

Focus: God Will Respond

The early church was committed to their assignment to actively share the gospel message. Their work was not without opposition. As they were commanded to stop, they utilized their greatest weapon. Gathering together with other believers, they cried out to the Lord. Their prayers were heard. God responded that all might see. Their work continued.

As you seek to do the will of the Lord, you will face opposition. It is key that you recognize the power of your prayers. Refusing to yield, turn to the Lord and pray. He will respond on your behalf. His work must go forth.

Day 262

Acts 4:13 Now when they saw the boldness of Peter and John, and perceived that they were unlearned and ignorant men, they marvelled; and they took knowledge of them, that they had been with Jesus.

Thought: They Had Been With Jesus

Focus: Relationship Requires Fellowship

Peter and John gained the attention of the High Priest and the rulers of the synagogue, as they proclaimed who Jesus was. They knew they had not been educated, but yet they spoke with boldness. What made the difference was that they had been with Jesus.

We often hear of the importance of one's relationship with Jesus. Acknowledging how important this is, we must also understand that without fellowship there will be no relationship. Insist on spending time with Jesus, a strong relationship will follow.

Day 263

Acts 3:6 Then Peter said, Silver and gold have I none; but such as I have give I thee: In the name of Jesus Christ of Nazareth rise up and walk.

Thought: You Have The Power (Through Christ) To Change Lives

Focus: As God Directs Follow

As Peter and John proceeded to the Temple for the hour of prayer, the Lord led them to a particular man who was there begging for alms. Peter spoke to the man, who had until then been unable to walk. As Peter assisted the man, his feet and ankle bones received strength. Leaping, he arose and began praising God. His life, through the prayers of Peter, was changed.

You have been empowered to change lives. The key is maintaining a relationship with the Lord that allows you to be sensitive to His Spirit. As He directs you, act in obedience. Through your obedience lives will be impacted.

Day 264

Acts 3:1 Now Peter and John went up together into the temple at the hour of prayer, being the ninth hour.

Thought: When It Is Time to Pray, Pray

Focus: Be Prepared To Listen

Prayer was a vital part of the early church. There were times set for prayer where all gathered to hear from God. Certainly, they made their requests known, but they were there mainly to hear from the Lord. When it was time to pray, they prayed.

How established is your prayer life? How is the bulk of your prayer time spent? For a growing relationship with the Lord, it is essential that you develop a consistent prayer life. Set a time daily that allows you to go before Him. He has much to share with you. When it is time to pray, pray.

Day 265

Acts 2:39 For the promise is unto you, and to your children, and to all that are afar off, even as many as the Lord our God shall call.

Thought: The Holy Ghost Was Not For Just That Day

Focus: Don't Allow Another's Doubt Hinder What God Has For You

After recognizing their error, those that had listened to Peter, asked what they should do. Peter responded by telling them to repent and be baptized. He did not limit, how God would respond, to just them. He explained that the promise was for all generations. The Holy Ghost was not just meant for that day.

As you interact with others, you will discover that many believe that what God did in the first century was just for then. The miracles, the signs and wonders, and the reception of the Holy Ghost, according to them, no longer takes place. The Bible tells us differently. God's gifts are for all generations. Don't allow the doubts of others hinder what God has for you.

Day 266

Acts 2:36-37 Therefore let all the house of Israel know assuredly, that God hath made that same Jesus, whom ye have crucified, both Lord and Christ. Now when they heard this, they were pricked in their heart, and said unto Peter and to the rest of the apostles, Men and brethren, what shall we do?

Thought: God's Word Has The Power To Change Hearts

Focus: The Truth Has The Power To Set You Free

As the multitude listened to Peter share the Word, many hearts were impacted. They now realized what they had done. They had crucified Jesus, the one that God had sent as Lord and Christ. God's Word had the power to change their hearts.

As you develop your relationship with the Lord, it is essential that you understand the power of God's Word. It is able to set you free from those areas of your life that yet need changing. Commit yourself to a study of the Word. It has the power to change your heart.

Day 267

Acts 2:16-17 But this is that which was spoken by the prophet Joel; And it shall come to pass in the last days, saith God, I will pour out of my Spirit upon all flesh: and your sons and your daughters shall prophesy, and your young men shall see visions, and your old men shall dream dreams:

Thought: Every God Given Prophecy Will Be Fulfilled

Focus: The Timing Is In His Hands

When the Jews, that had assembled from every nation for Pentecost, heard the 120 praising God and speaking in other tongues some stated they must be drunk. Peter stood up declaring that they were not drunk, but this was the fulfillment of Joel's prophecy. At the proper time, every God given prophecy will be fulfilled.

God's prophecies not only come to large groups of people, but also to individuals. If you have received a God given prophecy, it may not occur according to your timing, but it shall be fulfilled. The timing is in God's hands.

Day 268

Acts 1:8 But ye shall receive power, after that the Holy Ghost is come upon you: and ye shall be witnesses unto me both in Jerusalem, and in all Judaea, and in Samaria, and unto the uttermost part of the earth.

Thought: You Have Been Empowered To Witness

Focus: The Message Must Be Heard

As Jesus spoke of his leaving and the need for them to receive the promise of the Father, the thoughts of the disciples turned to natural things. They were quickly provided with what their assignment was. They were going to be empowered to carry the message of salvation; a message that all must hear.

When Jesus instructed his disciples, they were told to carry his message to all. The need for that remains today. You have been empowered, with the Holy Ghost, to be witnesses of salvation. As you were positioned to receive, you will now be positioned to share. The message must be heard by all.

Day 269

Acts 1:4 And, being assembled together with them, commanded them that they should not depart from Jerusalem, but wait for the promise of the Father, which, saith he, ye have heard of me.

Thought: Position Yourself To Receive

Focus: God Has Something Needed For Your Journey

As Jesus was about to ascend to his Father, he instructed his disciples to go to Jerusalem and wait. Their obedience was essential. The journey that was before them would require them to receive the promise of the Father. They were not to depart until the promise was fulfilled.

You have been chosen by the Lord to serve Him. Your journey will bring you many challenges for which you will need to be empowered. Position yourself both physically and spiritually, that you might receive the promise of the Father. He will equip you with what is needed for victory.

Day 270

Proverbs 19:11 The discretion of a man deferreth his anger; and it is his glory to pass over a transgression.

Thought: Sound Judgement Defers Anger

Focus: Every Battle Need Not Be Fought

The scriptures teach us to pursue peace. That this might occur, we must learn to defer anger. Every battle need not be fought. As we allow discretion to lead us, peace with others can be accomplished. The Lord has assured us that if our ways please Him, He would make even our enemies to be at peace with us.

It is a reality that others will initiate situations that inappropriately misuse you. When this occurs, do not be quick to allow anger to control your behavior. Allow discretion to take place, defer the anger, choosing rather to pursue peace. Every battle does not need to be fought.

Day 271

Matthew 21:21 Jesus answered and said unto them, Verily I say unto you, If ye have faith, and doubt not, ye shall not only do this which is done to the fig tree, but also if ye shall say unto this mountain, Be thou removed, and be thou cast into the sea; it shall be done.

Thought: Doubt Is Your Enemy; It Must Be Defeated

Focus: Faith Is Your Weapon Of Choice

The disciples of Jesus marveled after watching Jesus curse a fig tree. He responded by telling them that they could do even greater works. The key to their success was dependent on them having victory over doubt. If they would act in faith, success would occur.

Doubt questions what is possible and what is not. When you find yourself being challenged by doubt, faith is your greatest weapon. Place your trust in the Lord, act in faith, and watch God work.

Day 272

Matthew 14:16 But Jesus said unto them, They need not depart; give ye them to eat.

Thought: With Jesus, The Impossible Becomes Possible

Focus: As He Directs, Follow with Obedience

A great multitude followed Jesus into a desert place. When evening approached, his disciples encouraged him to send the people away that they might find food. After hearing their request, he directed the disciples to have the people remain. He then proceeded, with five fish and two loaves, to feed the thousands of men, women, and children. The impossible became possible.

You will face, in life, certain conditions that appear to have no solution. They will look to be impossible. Though with man that may be true, with God all things are possible. As He directs you, follow with obedience. Your need will be met.

Day 273

Philippians 3:14 I press toward the mark for the prize of the high calling of God in Christ Jesus.

Thought: Stay Focused on Where You Are Going

Focus: Let Nothing Deter Your Journey

Paul, on his journey with the Lord, acknowledged that he was not where he wanted to be. That he might continue forward, he let go of past failures and successes, and remained focused on his continued growth. He understood that opposition would come but was unwilling to have his journey deterred. He continued to press forward.

As you continue your growth in the Lord, be assured that you will face opposition. It will come from both within and without. As it does, do not allow it to deter your journey. Remain focused on going forward. There is a prize that awaits you.

Day 274

Matthew 6:24 No man can serve two masters: for either he will hate the one, and love the other; or else he will hold to the one, and despise the other. Ye cannot serve God and mammon.

Thought: God Or Riches; A Choice Must Be Made

Focus: No One Can Serve Two Masters

The scriptures teach us that where your treasure is your heart will be also. Choices in life are essential in all areas, especially in determining what is most important to us. Though it is true God has the ability to bless His children greatly, riches must not be the focal point of one's heart. The love for the Lord cannot have competition with anything; a choice must be made.

As you take a careful look at what drives you, are you driven to please God or are riches what determines your decision? It is essential that you understand that there can only be one master in your life. A choice must be made as to who you will serve. Be assured that if you choose the Lord that He will meet all of your needs. He is the proper and wise choice.

Day 275

1 John 5:3 For this is the love of God, that we keep his commandments: and his commandments are not grievous.

Thought: Because We Love We Obey

Focus: His Commandments Are Not Grievous; They Lead to Victory

Our increased knowledge of God changes both our perception of Him and our behavior. The more we know, the greater our appreciation for His concern for our wellbeing. What may have concerned us is no longer. We realize that His commandments are not grievous but there to lead us to victory.

Your thoughts of God's Word may have included some questions as why some were necessary. Those will change as your knowledge of Him increases. You will learn that all He commands is there to lead you to victory. His commandments are not grievous.

Day 276

Psalm 118:6 The LORD is on my side; I will not fear: what can man do unto me?

Thought: You Are Not Standing By Yourself

Focus: There Is No Need to Fear; The Lord Is on Your Side.

David speaks of his response when he finds himself in distress. There was no need for him to allow fear to overcome him. He called upon the Lord, with the assurance of knowing he was not standing by himself. With God on his side, there was nothing man could do.

It is essential that you understand that no matter what you face, the Lord is on your side. When periods of distress seek to usher in fear, call upon the one that holds your victory. Remind yourself there is nothing man can do to you. You are not standing by yourself.

Day 277

Job 42:5 I have heard of thee by the hearing of the ear: but now mine eye seeth thee.

Thought: Hearing Is Good Seeing Is Better

Focus: God Is About to Change Your Life Forever

Job's story is a powerful one. The attacks on his family, his treasure, and then his body, pushed him to a point of questioning where God was. When God did step in, Job saw a level of God's power that he previously had only heard about. It was an experience that changed his life forever. Hearing is good but seeing is better.

As you walk with God, you will hear about His wondrous working power. They will add to your knowledge of Him and your faith. As important as hearing is, when God reveals to you first hand, and allows you to see Him work, it will change your life forever. Hearing is good, seeing is better.

Day 278

Revelation 1:3 Blessed is he that readeth, and they that hear the words of this prophecy, and keep those things which are written therein: for the time is at hand.

Thought: Read, Hear, Obey

Focus: Today Not Tomorrow

As Jesus speaks to us through John, we are reminded of the importance of the words he shares. We are to read and hear the prophetic words that are to come, but most of all we must respond in obedience. Our commitment must not be pushed off to tomorrow but is needed today.

Too often, though we acknowledge what actions we are to take, our obedience is pushed off to tomorrow. As you read and hear the word of the Lord, your response cannot be delayed. Today, not tomorrow, is the time to say yes.

Day 279

Luke 8:24 And they came to him, and awoke him, saying, Master, master, we perish. Then he arose and rebuked the wind and the raging of the water: and they ceased, and there was a calm.

Thought: Your Storm Is No Match for Jesus

Focus: At His Command Calm Is Coming

Jesus took his disciples with him into a ship to travel to the other side. As they crossed the sea, a great storm arose. The disciples panicked as water began to fill the ship. They quickly woke Jesus, who had gone to sleep. As he rose, he rebuked the wind. As he did, all became calm. The storm was no match for Jesus.

In your life storms will arise. There is no need to panic. Simply call upon the one that has the power to calm the storm. Be assured that your storm is no match for the Lord. As He speaks, calm will follow.

Day 280

Ephesians 4:14 That we henceforth be no more children, tossed to and fro, and carried about with every wind of doctrine, by the sleight of men, and cunning craftiness, whereby they lie in wait to deceive;

Thought: Spiritual Maturity Is Demonstrated With Stable Behavior

Focus: Teachers Are Provided For Our Learning

God has given to his church gifted men and women to aid us in our growth process. He desires that we mature in our knowledge of God's Word, leading to stable Godly behavior. As we are taught, we must remain focused. It is essential that we come to a place in God that our actions consistently present a Godly life.

As others observe your life, do they see a life that presents Jesus? Is there a consistent growth process that has brought you to a place of spiritual maturity? It is essential that you come to that place in God where you are not susceptible to deceptive teachings. Spiritual maturity is a must.

Day 281

Psalm 30:5 For his anger endureth but a moment; in his favour is life: weeping may endure for a night, but joy cometh in the morning.

Thought: In The Midst of Your Tears Know That Joy Is Coming

Focus: Let The Praise Start Now

David encountered many challenges in his life. Both those that were close to him as well as the enemies of Israel sought his life. Amid his tears, David knew his God would intervene. His praise went forth knowing joy was coming.

You will face disappointment in your life. At those difficult times, be assured God has not forsaken you. Though the night might bring tears, let your praise go forth, for joy is coming in the morning.

Day 282

John 13:34-35 A new commandment I give unto you, that ye love one another; as I have loved you, that ye also love one another. By this shall all men know that ye are my disciples, if ye have love one to another.

Thought: The Trademark of The Church Is Its Love One for Another

Focus: Jesus Set the Example

One of the last conversations Jesus had with his disciples, prior to being taken by the soldiers, focused on the importance of them loving one another. It was not left for them to decide the importance of what he said, but it was given as a commandment. This would be the way others would know who they were, by their love of one for another.

The church is not to be like the world, a place where there is disregard one for another. It is to be a place where there is love one for another. It is through this love that others will know who the true followers of Jesus are.

Day 283

John 15:11 These things have I spoken unto you, that my joy might remain in you, and that your joy might be full.

Thought: There Is A Joy That Remains

Focus: Listen, Learn, And Obey

Jesus wanted his followers to understand the importance of his words. He taught them with intent, not to simply have something to do. It was through what he shared that they would gain true joy. As they learned and obeyed, they would discover true joy, joy that would remain.

Your search for joy need not go any further than the teachings of Jesus. As you carefully listen, and then obey, you will discover true joy. It is a joy that will remain with you, one that will make you full.

Day 284

1 Samuel 17:37 David said moreover, The LORD that delivered me out of the paw of the lion, and out of the paw of the bear, he will deliver me out of the hand of this Philistine. And Saul said unto David, Go, and the LORD be with thee.

Thought: Yesterday's Victory Produces Today's Faith

Focus: The Same God That Blessed Yesterday is able to Bless Today

David, as a young shepherd boy, faced both a lion and a bear. With the Lord's hand upon him, he defeated both. With this experience, he had the faith to challenge the giant Goliath. He understands that the same God that blessed then would bless again.

Your walk with God will produce experiences that reveal His power. Each occurrence is not to be seen as a single event, but a display of power that does not diminish. As you face your new challenges, be assured that the same God that blessed yesterday can bless again today.

Day 285

John 15:16 Ye have not chosen me, but I have chosen you, and ordained you, that ye should go and bring forth fruit, and that your fruit should remain: that whatsoever ye shall ask of the Father in my name, he may give it you.

Thought: Your Relationship Started With God

Focus: You've Been Chosen For God's Purpose

As Jesus spoke with his disciples, he reminded them that it was him that chose them, not them choosing him. They were chosen and ordained for his purpose, they were to go forth and bring forth fruit.

Your relationship with the Lord did not start with you. He chose you for His Will to be accomplished. You are to go forth and bring back fruit. You have been called for His purpose.

Day 286

Acts 19: And he said unto them, Unto what then were ye baptized? And they, said, Unto John's baptism.

Thought: There Is More Waiting On You

Focus: Remain Open to Continued Growth

As Paul's journey took him to Ephesus, he met with some believers who were Baptized following John but not Baptized in the name of Jesus Christ. When he questioned them if they had received the Holy Ghost since they believed, they responded that they had not even heard of that. Through their obedience to Paul's instructions they received the Holy Ghost, spoke in tongues, and prophesied. Their openness to growth was rewarded.

As you celebrate your relationship with God, remain aware that there is always more to gain. Your growth in God is a process. Through your experiences and study, God will consistently reveal more to you. Remain open to growth, there is yet more waiting on you.

Day 287

Acts 10:34-35 Then Peter opened his mouth, and said, Of a truth I perceive that God is no respecter of persons: But in every nation he that feareth him, and worketh righteousness, is accepted with him.

Thought: Salvation Is For Everyone

Focus: It Begins with The Proper Spirit

When the Holy Ghost fell on the Day of Pentecost, it was the followers of Jesus that were the recipients. They, and the three thousand that were added, were of the Jewish faith. It was their belief that others were not able to be included. It was through Peter carrying the message to Cornelius, a non-Jew, that the Lord made it known that salvation was for all. Those that had the proper spirit, and received the Word, would be added to the church. God is not a respecter of persons.

You have been blessed with the Word of God. As you share the message of salvation, do not decide who is able to receive it and who is not. One's background or former beliefs does not eliminate them from receiving God's Word. God is not a respecter of persons. With the right spirit, and an acceptance of the Word, salvation is available to all.

Day 288

Revelation 3:20 Behold, I stand at the door, and knock: if any man hear my voice, and open the door, I will come in to him, and will sup with him, and he with me.

Thought: There Is A Door Only You Can Open

Focus: Jesus Is Waiting To Enter

In the second and third chapters of the book of Revelation, John writes to the seven churches. His letter to the Laodiceans includes an appeal and an invitation to them. He tells them that he is at the door knocking, waiting for them to open it. When they respond, he will enter and sup with them. It is a door only they can open.

The Lord desires an intimate relationship with each of his sons and daughters, one that requires both quantity and quality time with Him. He remains knocking at your door, waiting for you to respond. It is a door only you can open. Respond now and enjoy all that He has to share.

Day 289

1 Samuel 3:9 Therefore Eli said unto Samuel, Go, lie down: and it shall be, if he call thee, that thou shalt say, Speak, LORD; for thy servant heareth. So Samuel went and lay down in his place.

Thought: God Is Speaking; Are You Listening?

Focus: Position Yourself To Hear

As Samuel was being trained to serve the Lord, there was a time he did not yet know the voice of God. He had gone to Eli, thinking it was him that called him. Eli, perceiving that it was God speaking, sent Samuel back to bed. He instructed him, that if he again heard God calling, reply stating, speak Lord, for thy servant heareth. He was positioned to hear His voice.

God has much each of us needs to hear. It is essential that you remain sensitive to His voice. Remain in a place that when He speaks, you are able to respond. Use the words of Samuel, speak Lord, for thy servant heareth. Position yourself that you might hear.

Day 290

Psalm 40:31 But they that wait upon the LORD shall renew their strength; they shall mount up with wings as eagles; they shall run, and not be weary; and they shall walk, and not faint.

Thought: As You Wait On The Lord Good Things Are Happening

Focus: While Others Faint, You Will Be Running

Life can be challenging, causing one to become weary. The key to a successful journey is learning how to wait on the Lord. As one's trust is placed in to His hands, there is no longer the limit of personal strength. It is through His strength, that while others faint, running is maintained.

Many become weary as they seek to serve the Lord. The challenges that come can be overwhelming as you seek to please Him. The key to your success is learning how to "wait on Him". As you do, He will renew your strength, allowing you to continue to run.

Day 291

Numbers 24:10 And Balak's anger was kindled against Balaam, and he smote his hands together: and Balak said unto Balaam, I called thee to curse mine enemies, and, behold, thou hast altogether blessed them these three times.

Thought: Whom God Blesses, No One Can Curse

Focus: As A Child Of God, You Are Blessed

Balak, King of the Moabites, hired Balaam to curse the people of Israel. Three times, though he started to curse them, he blessed them. When Balak challenged Balaam on what had occurred, he was told that no one can curse whom God has blessed.

As a child of God, God has blessed you. Your enemies may seek to curse you, but their efforts will be in vain. Whom the Lord blesses, no man can curse. Stay humble and walk in the Word; you will enjoy the blessings of the Lord. As a child of God, God has blessed you. Your enemies may seek to curse you, but their efforts will be in vain. Whom the Lord blesses, no man can curse. Stay humble and walk in the Word; you will enjoy the blessings of the Lord.

Day 292

2 Timothy 1:6 Wherefore I put thee in remembrance that thou stir up the gift of God, which is in thee by the putting on of my hands.

Thought: Your Gift Is Not To Stay Dormant

Focus: Others Are Waiting For You To Share

Paul understood the struggle that Timothy was facing. In order to encourage the younger man, he reminded him of the gift that was within him. It could not remain dormant, it needed to be stirred up. There was no need to fear those who opposed him. He had been empowered by God to bless multitudes.

The ability to bless others is not dependent on human power. The Lord has empowered His children with gifts that are to be used to bless others. These gifts cannot be allowed to sit dormant, they must be stirred up. Go forth and use what God has placed within you. Others are waiting to be blessed.

Day 293

3 John 1:2 Beloved, I wish above all things that thou mayest prosper and be in health, even as thy soul prospereth.

Thought: God Is Concerned About All Of You

Focus: Maintain Godly Priorities, God First, The Rest Will Follow.

John expresses to his readers his desire that their blessings flow into all aspects of their lives. Their health, their prosperity, all matter to the Lord. As we recognize this, we must not overlook what is the foundation of the list, as your soul prospers. Without spiritual health all else is meaningless. Our relationship with the Lord is the key.

The Lord wants you to be blessed in all things. Understanding that we must keep our priorities in order, begin your prayer seeking a strong spiritual focus. Let that be followed by sound health. The next in line would be the area of financial stability. As you start with Him first, the rest will follow.

Day 294

Luke 21:2-4 And he saw also a certain poor widow casting in thither two mites. And he said, Of a truth I say unto you, that this poor widow hath cast in more than they all: For all these have of their abundance cast in unto the offerings of God: but she of her penury hath cast in all the living that she had.

Thought: It Is The Spirit Not The Amount That Matters

Focus: Some Give Of Their Abundance, Others Give Their All

As Jesus watched as a number of those with wealth came to bring their gifts, he noted that they gave of their abundance. In contrast, a widow came and gave her last, two mites. Jesus commented, declaring that hers was the greater. It is the spirit not the amount that matters.

Giving is a spirit. Those that are blessed to be givers do not limit themselves to what they possess. They give to the need, trusting God to provide. Their gifts are not of their abundance, they give their all.

Day 295

Luke 21:19 In your patience possess ye your souls.

Thought: In The Midst of Your Storm, Remain Calm

Focus: There Is a Time, With Faith, To Wait

As Jesus shared with his followers, the challenges they would face, he stressed the need for patience. There thoughts must not be allowed to have them take unwarranted action. There is a time, with faith, to wait.

Panic can lead to poor decisions. Knowing that God has promised to turn your storm into your testimony, it is important that you remain calm. As you wait on the Lord, be assured that He will respond.

Day 296

Luke 21:12 But before all these, they shall lay their hands on you, and persecute you, delivering you up to the synagogues, and into prisons, being brought before kings and rulers for my name's sake. And it shall turn to you for a testimony.

Thought: The Enemy Is Seeking To Destroy You

Focus: Your Storm Will Become Your Testimony

As Jesus prepared his followers to carry the gospel message, he wanted them to know what they would face. The enemy, seeking to destroy them, would persecute them with some being placed in prison. They also needed to know that whatever they might face, God was with them. Their storms would become their testimonies.

As you continue to serve the Lord, telling others about His goodness, the enemy will seek to destroy you. As you face the various attacks, remain confident. God has it all under control. Your storm will soon become your testimony.

Day 297

Luke 19:47 And he taught daily in the temple. But the chief priests and the scribes and the chief of the people sought to destroy him.

Thought: In The Midst of Opposition, God's Work Must Continue

Focus: True Commitment Is Not Easily Stopped

During the last days of his life, Jesus continued to teach God's Word. Amid the opposition of the chief priests, he went daily into the Temple to teach. True commitment is not easily stopped.

The level of the commitment of someone can be measured when they face opposition. You will have those that feel your teaching should stop. Knowing what God has done for you, continue sharing the good news. His work must continue.

Day 298

Mark 11:15 And they come to Jerusalem: and Jesus went into the temple, and began to cast out them that sold and bought in the temple, and overthrew the tables of the moneychangers, and the seats of them that sold doves;

Thought: God's House Is A House Of Prayer, Not A Den Of Thieves

Focus: The Focus Must Remain On God And Godly Things

Throughout the ministry of Jesus, during his three years, we only see him taking strong action on one occasion. As he entered the Temple, he began to overthrow the tables, casting out those who had turned his Father's house of prayer into a den of thieves. The focus was no longer on God and Godly things.

It is essential that we treat God's house properly. It is a place that we assemble to worship the Lord as well as spend time in prayer. It is not a place to take advantage of others for personal gain. As you enter the House of the Lord, insist on maintaining your focus on God and Godly things.

Day 299

Mark 11:7 And they brought the colt to Jesus, and cast their garments on him; and he sat upon him.

Thought: In Meekness He Entered Jerusalem

Focus: As He Was Humble; We Are to Be Humble

When it was time to enter Jerusalem, leading to his crucifixion, Jesus chose to enter in a manner of humility. It was on a colt that he rode as they cried Hosanna, Hosanna. Throughout all his ministry, Jesus practiced humility. As he was humble, so should our lives be also.

The walk of a child of God, regardless of their title or position, should be one of humility. As you seek to follow the Lord, do so as he did. He never sought the high place or to surround himself with riches. He remained humble. Let your life demonstrate the same.

Day 300

Romans 6:1-2 What shall we say then? Shall we continue in sin, that grace may abound? God forbid. How shall we, that are dead to sin, live any longer therein?

Thought: Grace Is Not an Excuse To Sin

Focus: Stay Focused on Living Holy

Understanding the importance of God's grace in our lives is essential. We know that we are saved not by works, but by His grace. As we celebrate His grace, it is vital that we must not see this as an excuse to sin. Our focus must be on living in accordance with God's Word.

We serve a God who is long suffering with us. It is by His grace that we can continue our journey. As you celebrate His grace, it is key that you do not see it as a license to sin. Stay focused on living holy that the Lord might be glorified in your life.

Day 301

2 Corinthians 4:8-9 We are troubled on every side, yet not distressed; we are perplexed, but not in despair; Persecuted, but not forsaken; cast down, but not destroyed;

Thought: Challenges Yes; Defeat No

Focus: With God You Are Victorious

Paul's ministry was powerful, with multitudes coming to know God. He ministered to the rich, to the poor, to the powerful, and to the common man. As he shared, he faced many challenges. He speaks of persecutions as well as trouble, but in all that he faced, he remained victorious. With God leading and directing, he could not be defeated.

As you seek to share the gospel, you will find opposition. There will be challenges to what you are doing, but you must remain positive. Be assured, as you follow God's directions, you will always be victorious.

Day 302

Matthew 9:28-29 And when he was come into the house, the blind men came to him: and Jesus saith unto them, Believe ye that I am able to do this? They said unto him, Yea, Lord. Then touched he their eyes, saying, According to your faith be it unto you.

Thought: Seek The One That Can Change Your Situation

Focus: Your Faith Is The Difference Maker

Two blind men, determined to be healed, sought Jesus. They were assured that he had the power to restore their sight. As they approached him, he questioned their faith. They affirmed that he was able. He touched their eyes and they received their sight. Their faith made the difference.

Many approach Jesus with a variety of reasons. Some come with faith, while others are uncertain. As one that knows the Word, do not allow doubt to overshadow your faith. With determination, and belief, seek the one that is able. Your faith will make the difference, your request will be honored.

Day 303

Joshua 7:5 And the men of Ai smote of them about thirty and six men: for they chased them from before the gate even unto Shebarim, and smote them in the going down: wherefore the hearts of the people melted, and became as water.

Though: Sin Has Consequences

Focus: Disobedience Is Sin

After a victorious encounter at Jericho, Joshua expected no problems as they sought to defeat Ai. A smaller number of men were sent with expectations of an easy victory. They were totally surprised when they were met with defeat. They were unaware that the sin of disobedience had taken place during the conquest of Jericho. They were being taught the consequences of sin.

When God provides His children directions, He expects them to be followed. No part of His instructions can be regarded as unimportant. As God provides you with instructions, respond with total obedience. Obedience brings blessings while sin has its consequences.

Day 304

Psalm 30:5 For his anger endureth but a moment; in his favour is life: weeping may endure for a night, but joy cometh in the morning.

Thought: It May Be Challenging Tonight But Joy Is Soon To Come

Focus: With The Morning There Will Be Joy

In the midst of difficult times, it is essential that we remember the promises of God. He has committed Himself, even in His anger, that joy will follow the night of weeping. His love for His people will override His anger. It may be challenging during the night, but joy is soon to come.

Your behavior may have caused God to respond with anger, but be assured it is just for a moment. His love for you will bring an end to the weeping. With the morning there will be joy.

Day 305

1 John 4:20 If a man say, I love God, and hateth his brother, he is a liar: for he that loveth not his brother whom he hath seen, how can he love God whom he hath not seen?

Thought: Those That Love God Love Their Brother

Focus: Love Is More Than An Emotion

It is important that we understand what love is. It is more than an emotion but rather how we treat one another. Love is demonstrated by behavior that is in the best interest of others. As the Lord loves us we must love one another.

As you give thought to how you treat others ask yourself, am I demonstrating love? Are my actions taken because I care about the best interest of others? As God's love flows through you, your behavior must reflect the same. Those that love God, love their brothers.

Day 306

1 Corinthians 15:58 Therefore, my beloved brethren, be ye stedfast, unmoveable, always abounding in the work of the Lord, forasmuch as ye know that your labour is not in vain in the Lord.

Thought: Stay Focused, You Are Doing An Excellent Job

Focus: Your Efforts Are Not In Vain

As one faces the many obstacles that occur in ministry, there is the temptation to feel defeated. Paul writes providing the evidence that this is not true. He exhorts all to remain steadfast in their labor, with the assurance that their labor is not in vain. The Lord is aware of their efforts which shall prove to be fruitful.

Your commitment to the Kingdom has not gone unnoticed by God. As you labor in His will, be assured much is being accomplished. During those waiting times remain focused. Your labor is not in vain.

Day 307

Luke 4:2 Being forty days tempted of the devil. And in those days he did eat nothing: and when they were ended, he afterward hungered.

Thought: The Enemy Knows Where To Attack

Focus: Your Commitment To Prayer And The Word Is Essential

The scripture informs us that Jesus was led by the Spirit into the wilderness. After he had spent forty days fasting, Satan came to tempt him. Knowing that Jesus was now hungry, he tempted him to turn the rocks into bread. He knew where he was the most vulnerable.

As you continue your walk with the Lord, be assured that temptations will occur. They will be targeted at those areas where it appears that you are most vulnerable. It is important that you maintain a close walk with the Lord. Your continued commitment to prayer and the Word is essential.

Day 308

Isaiah 38:1-2 In those days was Hezekiah sick unto death. And Isaiah the prophet the son of Amoz came unto him, and said unto him, Thus saith the LORD, Set thine house in order: for thou shalt die, and not live. Then Hezekiah turned his face toward the wall, and prayed unto the LORD.

Thought: Every No Does Not Have To Be Accepted

Focus: Turn Your Face To The Wall And Weep

Hezekiah was told by the prophet to put his house in order. God has sent the message that he would not be healed, he was going to die. Hezekiah knew not to complain to the prophet, he turned his face to the wall and wept before God. The Lord responded and added fifteen years to his life.

No can be a hard answer to accept, especially when sent from God. When it is not acceptable, place your focus on the only one that can help. Turn your face to the wall and weep before God. He alone has the power to correct your situation.

Day 309

Psalm 32:8-9 I will instruct thee and teach thee in the way which thou shalt go: I will guide thee with mine eye. Be ye not as the horse, or as the mule, which have no understanding: whose mouth must be held in with bit and bridle, lest they come near unto thee.

Thought: As The Lord Instructs; Follow

Focus: Maintain A Spirit Of Obedience

David reminds us of the importance of having a spirit that freely responds to the instruction of the Lord. As He provides direction, a positive response is essential. Those with understanding gladly obey.

As a child of God, you will receive instruction from the Lord. He will provide you information that will lead you to victory. Be not as a mule or horse that has no understanding, but with a spirit of obedience, go forward as the Lord leads.

Day 310

Deuteronomy 28:2 And all these blessings shall come on thee, and overtake thee, if thou shalt hearken unto the voice of the LORD thy God.

Thought: God's Blessings Await You

Focus: Obedience Is Your Key To Victory

As Israel's journey through the wilderness neared an end, Moses stood before the people and shared what God intended for them. They would not just inherit the land, but would be blessed beyond measure. Their obedience was their key to victory.

It is God's will to bless you. He has taken you through your own personal wilderness, to prepare you to receive what He intends for you. As you have journeyed, He has demonstrated His ability to provide and protect. As He now directs your steps, you will discover that your obedience is the key to victory. Obey and be blessed.

Day 311

Daniel 10:12 Then said he unto me, Fear not, Daniel: for from the first day that thou didst set thine heart to understand, and to chasten thyself before thy God, thy words were heard, and I am come for thy words.

Thought: Fear Not; Your Prayer Has Been Heard

Focus: Your Sacrifices Are Not In Vain

Daniel was shown a vision, by the Lord, but did not have a full understanding of what he saw. With confidence, Daniel, through prayer and fasting, pursued the Lord for the clarity of the vision. For twenty-one days he cried, but there was no response. At the end of the three weeks, an angel appeared to Daniel and informed him that his prayer was heard, and a response was coming. His sacrifices were not offered in vain.

There will be times, in your journey, that it may appear that your prayers and fasting are not having an impact. Be assured, though there may be delays, God has heard your cries. Your sacrifices have not been offered in vain. Your answer is coming.

Day 312

1 Peter 1:14-16 As obedient children, not fashioning yourselves according to the former lusts in your ignorance: But as he which hath called you is holy, so be ye holy in all manner of conversation; Because it is written, Be ye holy; for I am holy.

Thought: In Obedience; We Are To Walk Holy

Focus: A Holy God Has Holy Followers

Peter reminds us that who we were yesterday cannot be who we are today. With a spirit of obedience, now being aware of the lusts that drove us yesterday, we are to walk holy. The word declares that those that seek to follow a Holy God must be holy.

As you look back at your life, you will recognize that in your ignorance, your walk did not always please God. You sought to satisfy the lusts that influenced you. Now that you are seeking to follow God, a change must be evident. Commit yourself to a holy conversation for God is an Holy God.

Day 313

Psalm 28:6-7 Blessed be the LORD, because he hath heard the voice of my supplications. The LORD is my strength and my shield; my heart trusted in him, and I am helped: therefore my heart greatly rejoiceth; and with my song will I praise him.

Thought: In The Midst Of Your Distress Cry Out To The Lord; He Will Respond

Focus: He Is Your Strength And Your Shield

David, in the midst of being attacked by his enemies, cried out to the Lord for help. As he pleaded his case, the Lord responded delivering His servant from those who sought to destroy him. David offered praise to the one that was his strength and his shield.

How does one respond when you come under attack from your enemies? One could yield, believing there is no hope, or they could seek the Lord's help. As you with confidence, choose the latter, you will discover a God that will respond. As you put your trust in the Lord, you will learn that He is your strength and your shield.

Day 314

1 Peter 2:1-2 Wherefore laying aside all malice, and all guile, and hypocrisies, and envies, and all evil speakings, As newborn babes, desire the sincere milk of the word, that ye may grow thereby:

Thought: A New You Is Being Formed

Focus: The Old Shall Be Replaced With The New

As Peter addresses the believer, he reminds them of the changes that are now expected in their lives. Malice, hypocrisy, and evil speaking can no longer be a part of who they are. They must all be laid aside, as they grow through their desire for God's Word. A new person is being formed.

As you entered the Kingdom of God, you brought who you were with you. Through your desire for God's Word, growth will take place. You will lay aside those things that do not represent God or who you now are. You are becoming the new person God called you to be.

Day 315

Philippians 3:14 I press toward the mark for the prize of the high calling of God in Christ Jesus.

Thought: Your Race Will Demand a Persistent Spirit

Focus: Stay Focused on The Mark; Let Nothing Deter You

Paul speaks of his determination to arrive at the place God has for him and for others. Recognizing there will be opposition, he is committed to press his way. He remains focused, allowing nothing to deter his efforts.

As we have started a period of sacrifice, seeking to draw nigh to the Lord, it is essential that we understand that there will be opposition. As you remain focused on the mark that is before you, commit yourself to press forward. Let nothing deter your journey.

Day 316

Matthew 18:21-22 Then came Peter to him, and said, Lord, how oft shall my brother sin against me, and I forgive him? till seven times? Jesus saith unto him, I say not unto thee, Until seven times: but, Until seventy times seven.

Thought: Forgiveness Has No Limits

Focus: As God Forgives Us; Let Us Forgive One Another

As Jesus was instructing his disciples, he was asked about forgiveness by Peter. If my brother offends me seven times must I still forgive him? Jesus responded by telling Peter if one offends you seventy times seven forgiveness remains in order. As God forgives us, we are to forgive one another. The spirit of forgiveness belongs in every believer's life.

You will be faced with situations, when you will be offended by inappropriate behavior, it is essential that you respond in a spiritual manner. Giving thought to how God continues to forgive you, regardless of the number of times you offend Him with ungodly behavior, forgiveness must be extended by you. A spirit of forgiveness belongs in your heart.

Day 317

James 4:8 Draw nigh to God, and he will draw nigh to you. Cleanse your hands, ye sinners; and purify your hearts, ye double minded.

Thought: Change Is A Part Of Drawing Nigh

Focus: What Needs To Go Needs To Go

The Word shares the promise of God to those that would draw nigh to Him. He in return will draw nigh to them. The scripture also gives thought to the need of letting go of those things that hinder our walk with the Lord. Drawing nigh requires letting go of all that separates us from the Lord. What needs to go needs to go.

As you spend time in prayer, during the Lenten season, God will speak with you. As a caring God, He will share with you those things that hinder your walk with Him. As you seek to draw nigh to Him, understand there will be a need to let go of anything that hinders your relationship with Him. He is waiting on you to draw nigh.

Day 318

Luke 4:1-2 And Jesus being full of the Holy Ghost returned from Jordan, and was led by the Spirit into the wilderness, Being forty days tempted of the devil. And in those days he did eat nothing: and when they were ended, he afterward hungered.

Thought: You Will Be Attacked: Preparation Is Essential

Focus: Preparation Includes Sacrifice

Many followers of Jesus, beginning tomorrow, will spend the next weeks observing the Lenten season. It is a time to reflect on the sacrifice Jesus endured, when led by the Spirit into the wilderness. Knowing what challenges were before him, he understood that he must be prepared and that sacrifices were a necessary part of his preparation.

Living for the Lord includes an understanding that you will face spiritual attacks. The enemy remains committed to separating you from the Lord. It is essential that you prepare yourself for these attacks. Understanding that your preparation will include sacrifices, do not make the mistake of doing too much or too little. As the Spirit leads, follow.

Day 319

Genesis 15:1 After these things the word of the LORD came unto Abram in a vision, saying, Fear not, Abram: I am thy shield, and thy exceeding great reward.

Thought: God Honors Those That Put Their Trust Into His Hands

Focus: God Is Your Provider And Protector

As Abram journeyed, in obedience to the Lord, his trust continued to mature. His focus for all of his needs was placed into the hands of the Lord. In response, the Lord reminded His servant that He was His shield and great reward. He would be His provider and His protector.

As you place your trust into the Lord's hand, you will learn that He is able to meet all of your needs. With faith, walk in obedience to His commands. He will be your shield and great reward. He will provide for your needs and protect you from your enemies.

Day 320

Genesis 13:14-15 And the LORD said unto Abram, after that Lot was separated from him, Lift up now thine eyes, and look from the place where thou art northward, and southward, and eastward, and westward: For all the land which thou seest, to thee will I give it, and to thy seed for ever.

Thought: The Lord Seeks Total Obedience

Focus: A Great Reward Awaits You

When Abram was yet in Ur, the Lord directed him to leave, taking only his wife with him. Abram did leave, but also brought his nephew and father with him. His journey included a stop in Haran as well as in Egypt. It was not until he was separated from his nephew, and in the land God had spoken of, that he received the promise. His total obedience resulted in a great reward.

There are promises that God shares with His children that are without conditions, while others have conditions that must be met. When there are conditions, God is expecting total obedience. As you come to that place of obedience, you will be in position to receive all that God intends for your life. Your obedience will result in a great reward.

Day 321

Hebrews 10:36 For ye have need of patience, that, after ye have done the will of God, ye might receive the promise.

Thought: Remain Patient As You Continue Forward

Focus: Your Confidence Will Result In Great Rewards

The scripture helps us to understand the importance of patience. As the saint remains in the will of God, doubt cannot be allowed to push back their faith. With confidence, one must patiently wait with the assurance of great rewards resulting.

As you continue in the will of God, you will learn that there is the need of patience. During those times of waiting, remain both patient and confident. You can be assured that your commitment to doing the will of the Lord will result in you receiving the promise. Great results are coming.

Day 322

Exodus 14:21 And Moses stretched out his hand over the sea; and the LORD caused the sea to go back by a strong east wind all that night, and made the sea dry land, and the waters were divided.

Thought: Your Enemy Is Subject To God

Focus: When God Commands All Must Obey

In what was an apparent defeat for Israel, God demonstrated His power on their behalf. As Moses obeyed the Lord's instructions and stretched his hand across the sea, the Lord ordered the wind to move the waters back. The sea was now divided and the land was dry.

It is a fact that the enemy desires to kill, steal, and destroy. Though he will endeavor to use whatever method he can muster against you, he remains subject to God. Stay confident, for as you remain focused on God you need not yield or compromise. Your safety is assured.

Day 323

Exodus 14:14 The LORD shall fight for you, and ye shall hold your peace.

Thought: Stay Calm; God Is In Control

Focus: The Battle Is In God's Hand

It appeared that Egypt had Israel cornered in with no pathway to escape. Their future looked doomed. In the midst of apparent defeat, Moses spoke out declaring all is well. They should hold their peace; the Lord would fight for them.

You have faced situations that seemed hopeless, with you ready to simply give up. It is at those times that the Lord is saying, stay calm, the battle is His to fight. As you place your trust in the Lord you will learn everything, including your enemy is under His control.

Day 324

James 1:5 If any of you lack wisdom, let him ask of God, that giveth to all men liberally, and upbraideth not; and it shall be given him.

Though: Wisdom Awaits Your Request

Focus: Ask And You Shall Receive

In the book of Proverbs we are told of the importance of wisdom. Solomon declares that it is the principal thing, it must be sought. James instructs us to ask, with confidence, knowing that the Lord giveth liberally to all those that ask. Wisdom awaits our request.

In your walk with God, you will encounter many situations where earthly wisdom is not sufficient. Recognizing our need, God has made His wisdom available to all that ask. Follow the counsel of James, ask and you shall receive.

Day 325

Matthew 11:28-30 Come unto me, all ye that labour and are heavy laden, and I will give you rest. Take my yoke upon you, and learn of me; for I am meek and lowly in heart: and ye shall find rest unto your souls. For my yoke is easy, and my burden is light.

Thought: Rest For Your Soul Awaits You

Focus: The More You Learn The Greater The Rest

Jesus, as he taught the people, gave an invitation to all. Those that would come unto him would find rest. As they would learn of the Lord, they would recognize that his yoke is easy and his burden is light.

Life has its many challenges. It can cause one to become overwhelmed with all that they may encounter. In the midst of those struggles, an invitation has been extended. As you recognize that you are not able to handle all that you face, accept the Lord's invitation. You will find rest for your soul.

Day 326

Ephesians 4:1 I therefore, the prisoner of the Lord, beseech you that ye walk worthy of the vocation wherewith ye are called.

Thought: With The Proper Spirit, Your Assignment Is To Be Fulfilled

Focus: Seek To Maintain A Spirit Of Unity

Each child of God has been given an individual assignment. As they go forth to fulfill their assignment, it must be done with the proper spirit. With lowliness and meekness, demonstrating love one for another, the work must take place. A spirit of unity is to be maintained.

As a child of God, you have been given an assignment that is to be fulfilled. It is essential, that as you commit yourself to the task, you do so with a spirit of lowliness and meekness. As you demonstrate your love to others, you will be assisting in preserving a spirit of unity.

Day 327

1 Corinthians 2:9-10 But as it is written, Eye hath not seen, nor ear heard, neither have entered into the heart of man, the things which God hath prepared for them that love him. But God hath revealed them unto us by his Spirit: for the Spirit searcheth all things, yea, the deep things of God.

Thought: There Is Much Yet To See

Focus: What The Eye Cannot See The Spirit Shall Reveal

God has much to share with His followers. While there are surface items easily seen, the deep things can only be revealed by the Spirit. The natural man is limited to what he can see or hear. Only those that walk in the Spirit can receive the deep things of God.

The scripture shares the limitation of what the natural man can receive from God. What the eye cannot see and what the ear cannot hear, can only be received by the Spirit. Through a committed life of prayer, position yourself to receive what only the Spirit can reveal. The deep things await you.

Day 328

Nehemiah 1:4 And it came to pass, when I heard these words, that I sat down and wept, and mourned certain days, and fasted, and prayed before the God of heaven.

Thought: In The Midst Of Great Need; Pray

Focus: God Has The Answer To Your Question

When Nehemiah was told of the state of Jerusalem, he knew something had to be done but was uncertain as what could be accomplished. In the midst of his uncertainty, he did what needed to be done; he prayed. God responded.

There will be situations in your life that clearly require action to be taken. The challenge is when you don't know what that action should be. When facing that dilemma, the key is prayer. With determination go before the Lord, knowing that He will respond. The road to victory will be sent.

Day 329

Daniel 1:8 But Daniel purposed in his heart that he would not defile himself with the portion of the king's meat, nor with the wine which he drank: therefore he requested of the prince of the eunuchs that he might not defile himself.

Thought: What Begins In The Heart Must Be Shown In Behavior

Focus: Your Faith Will Not Lead You To Disappointment

Daniel, when told what the King directed them to be fed, purposed in his heart, not to defile himself. His determination was followed by his request to have only pulse and water. His faith was strong enough to trust God for victory; Daniel was not disappointed.

One's faith will be tested. It sounds encouraging when one speaks of their commitment to God's Word, but it must pass the test when challenged. As you purpose in your heart to walk with God, you need not fear; your faith will be honored.

Day 330

Colossians 4:5-6 Walk in wisdom toward them that are without, redeeming the time. Let your speech be always with grace, seasoned with salt, that ye may know how ye ought to answer every man.

Thought: Soul Winning Necessitates Wisdom

Focus: Let Grace Drive Your Conversation

Those that know God have the responsibility and privilege to lead others to Him. Success in this endeavor requires wisdom; knowing what and when to share is vital. The choice and the timing of the words used can mean the difference in either winning or simply offending a soul. Let grace drive your conversation.

In endeavoring to win a soul, have you ever spoken too quickly or perhaps too harshly? Wisdom dictates the need for grace in your conversations. Be prepared to answer any question that may be asked but do it with love and patience. Your goal is to bless not offend.

Day 331

Psalm 46:1 God is our refuge and strength, a very present help in trouble.

Thought: In The Midst Of Trouble Know Where To Turn

Focus: God Is Your Refuge

Trouble comes to all, the key is knowing where to turn when it arrives. The psalmist assures us that no matter what we may face, God is our present help. There is no need to fear, turn to the one that is your refuge.

In your most challenging times, there is no need to fear. You have a God that is always available. Turn to the one that is a very present help in the time of trouble. He is your place of safety; He is your refuge.

Day 332

Luke 5:4 Now when he had left speaking, he said unto Simon, Launch out into the deep, and let down your nets for a draught.

Thought: Allow Your Faith To Extend Your Reach

Focus: There Are Greater Blessings Yet To Come

Peter, and the other fishermen, had toiled all night and caught nothing. Though they were both tired and disappointed, Jesus instructed them to launch out again, this time further from shore. Their faith and obedience were being stretched. They obeyed and were successful.

Your faith will be tested. Your current reach will produce limited success. It is time to stretch your faith, as you share the gospel message. As the Lord directs, go beyond your current reach, you will discover greater rewards.

Day 333

Isaiah 40:31 But they that wait upon the LORD shall renew their strength; they shall mount up with wings as eagles; they shall run, and not be weary; and they shall walk, and not faint.

Thought: Wait On The Lord; He Will Strengthen You

Focus: Your Strength Is In God

As Isaiah presents the qualities of a God that never tires, he instructs Israel to put their trust in this same God. While others tire and faint, they will not. Those that wait on the Lord will run and not be weary, they will walk and not faint.

The key, as you journey, is to put your trust in God. Your ability to go forward is dependent on you waiting on Him. As you wait, you will be strengthened by a God who never sleeps or tires. He gives power to the weak, and to those that have no might He increases strength.

Day 334

Isaiah 41:10 Fear thou not; for I am with thee: be not dismayed; for I am thy God: I will strengthen thee; yea, I will help thee; yea, I will uphold thee with the right hand of my righteousness.

Thought: There Is No Need To Fear

Focus: God Is Your Help; He Will Strengthen You

The threat of other nations seeking to attack Israel was a constant threat. In the midst of these threats, God spoke to His people, reminding them that there was no need to fear. He was their help; He would uphold them.

Life brings many challenges, which can cause fear to arise within the child of God. Questions will arise; do I have the strength to go forward? At those times, it is needful to hear the voice of the Lord. He has promised to be with you; to strengthen you for your journey. He is your help.

Day 335

Deuteronomy 31:6 Be strong and of a good courage, fear not, nor be afraid of them: for the LORD thy God, he it is that doth go with thee; he will not fail thee, nor forsake thee.

Thought: Your Enemy Is Not Your Problem

Focus: Fear And Doubt Must Be Defeated

As the journey through the wilderness neared an end, God had Moses to share His message with the people. They were reminded that the Lord was with them, and that there was no need to fear the people that they would encounter. They were to be strong and of good courage. God had given them the land, victory was assured.

As God leads you to the fulfillment of His promise, there will be obstacles that appear to hinder your journey. As you encounter them, it is essential that you remain strong and of good courage. You have nothing to fear, God has given you the victory.

Day 336

Matthew 9:20-21 And, behold, a woman, which was diseased with an issue of blood twelve years, came behind him, and touched the hem of his garment: For she said within herself, If I may but touch his garment, I shall be whole.

Thought: Wholeness Is Just A Touch Away

Focus: Press Your Way; You Will Not Be Disappointed

Twelve years is a long time to struggle with a serious health issue, especially when no one offers any hope for healing. The woman with the issue of blood, being led by God, was convinced that her healing was simply a touch away. Against all odds, she pressed her way to touch the hem of the Lord's garment. As she did, she was made whole.

Regardless of the severity and duration of the condition you are facing, wholeness awaits you. While others cannot provide your deliverance, one touch with the Lord has the power to change everything. Press your way, you will not be disappointed.

Day 337

Hebrews 12:1 Wherefore seeing we also are compassed about with so great a cloud of witnesses, let us lay aside every weight, and the sin which doth so easily beset us, and let us run with patience the race that is set before us.

Thought: You've Been Assigned A Race; It Must Be Run

Focus: Avoid Distractions; Run With Patience

In the 11th chapter of Hebrews a list of men and women of faith are presented. Each one ran the race that God ordained for their life. Discarding everything that would hinder their journey, with faith, and patience, they successfully ran their race.

As those in chapter eleven, each of us has a race to run. That you might successfully complete your race, it is essential that you lay aside each weight that would hinder you. Then with faith, and patience, continue on. Your race must be run.

Day 338

Acts 13:2 As they ministered to the Lord, and fasted, the Holy Ghost said, Separate me Barnabas and Saul for the work whereunto I have called them.

Thought: God Is Speaking; Are You Listening

Focus: Position Yourself To Hear

As a certain number of the church leaders gave themselves to prayer and fasting, God spoke to them. They were instructed to send forth Paul and Barnabas to go forth to carry the word. They heard and obeyed. They had been positioned to hear.

As we understand that the Lord, not man, is the head of the church, we must position ourselves to hear what He is saying. Give yourself to prayer and fasting that you might be positioned to hear what He is saying. As you hear, obey.

Day 339

2 Corinthians 1:4 Who comforteth us in all our tribulation, that we may be able to comfort them which are in any trouble, by the comfort wherewith we ourselves are comforted of God.

Thought: As God Has Comforted Us We Are To Comfort Others

Focus: You Have Been Prepared To Bless

Moments of disappointment come to all. The child of God is blessed, during these trying times, to have a God who comforts them. Through the comfort they experienced, they will be able then to comfort others in the midst of their challenges. They have been prepared to bless others.

No one escapes the challenges that life brings. Even in those difficult times, you are being prepared by God to be able to bless others. As He comforts you, you will be able to comfort others as they face the challenges of life.

You have been prepared to bless.

Day 340

Mark 10:45 For even the Son of man came not to be ministered unto, but to minister, and to give his life a ransom for many.

Thought: You Have Been Called To Serve

Focus: Elevation Brings Responsibility

As the time for Jesus's departure became close, the disciples began to seek positions of authority. It provided a time for Jesus to share the responsibility of those that lead; they are to minister to others not to be ministered to. The pattern was set by Jesus. He came to suffer and die for the people.

Those that seek elevation must understand what they are asking for. As Jesus suffered for us, those in positions of authority must have the same spirit. They are to seek to serve rather than to be served. It is their responsibility.

Day 341

Ephesians 4:1 I therefore, the prisoner of the Lord, beseech you that ye walk worthy of the vocation wherewith ye are called, With all lowliness and meekness, with longsuffering, forbearing one another in love;

Thought: You Have An Assignment That Must Be Fulfilled

Focus: With Love And Humility Walk Worthy Of Your Calling

Paul shares with his readers the importance of their walk with the Lord. Every saint has an assignment that must be fulfilled. That it might be effective, humility and love are essential. Meekness and long suffering must be evident, with love being demonstrated one to another.

You have an assignment, given by God, for the betterment of the body of Christ. It is essential that you seek to fulfill it with the proper spirit. Your walk must be with lowliness and meekness. Your assignment must be properly fulfilled with love and humility.

Day 342

Colossians 3:8-10 But now ye also put off all these; anger, wrath, malice, blasphemy, filthy communication out of your mouth. Lie not one to another, seeing that ye have put off the old man with his deeds; And have put on the new man, which is renewed in knowledge after the image of him that created him:

Thought: The Old Must Die That The New Might Live

Focus: Let Your Life Demonstrate Who Jesus Is

As God brings one from darkness into the light, a change in one's behavior must take place. Anger, malice, and filthy communications all must no longer be a part of that life. The new walk must demonstrate who Jesus is. As he walked, so must we.

A new you, that must be the desire of every child of God. Your past must remain in the past and not brought into the present. Let your life testify of the new you God has created you to be. Let your life demonstrate who Jesus is.

Day 343

Ephesians 3:20 Now unto him that is able to do exceeding abundantly above all that we ask or think, according to the power that worketh in us.

Thought: You Have Been Empowered To Make A Difference

Focus: God Has Chosen To Work Through You

There are two important facts presented, by Paul, in this one verse. We serve a God that has the power to work beyond even our imagination is the first. The second, often overlooked, declares that He works through the power that is within us. The believer has been empowered to make a difference.

While we understand that the source of all power is God. He is the one that controls all things. It is vital that we also know, that He works through the believer. You have been empowered, by God, to make a difference.

Day 344

2 Timothy 1:6 Wherefore I put thee in remembrance that thou stir up the gift of God, which is in thee by the putting on of my hands.

Thought: Your Gift Must Not Remain Dormant

Focus: Others Are Waiting To Be Blessed

In Paul's letter to Timothy, he reminds the younger man of the importance of the gift that is within him. It must not remain dormant; it must be utilized. Timothy is instructed to stir up the gift that others may be blessed through it.

Gifts are given that other lives may be impacted. The gift that lies within you must not lie dormant. Stir it up that it might be properly used. Others are waiting to be blessed.

Day 345

Psalm 18:3 I will call upon the LORD, who is worthy to be praised: so shall I be saved from mine enemies.

Thought: With Praise And Confidence Call Upon The Lord

Focus: He Will Deliver You From Your Enemies

David faced many challenges. His life was threatened by Saul and his other enemies. David's response was to call upon the one who was worthy of his praise. As he cried out to the Lord, he was confident that he would be delivered. He was not disappointed.

Maintaining your focus on God is essential at all times. Do not allow any situation to cause you to lose sight of the one that is worthy of your praise. When you find yourself under attack, call upon the Lord. He will deliver you from your enemies.

Day 346

Isaiah 43:2 When thou passest through the waters, I will be with thee; and through the rivers, they shall not overflow thee: when thou walkest through the fire, thou shalt not be burned; neither shall the flame kindle upon thee.

Though: Storms Will Come, But They Will Not Destroy You

Focus: With God, As Your Protector, You Are Coming Out Victorious

Isaiah makes it clear, storms will occur in the lives of all of God's people. All will pass through the waters and will walk through the fire. In the midst of those challenging times, there is the joy of knowing that God is the protector. The waters will not overflow the saint nor will the fire burn them. They will come out victorious.

In your walk with the Lord, you will face challenging times. As you do, you need not fear. Neither the waters or the fire will harm thee. With God, as your protector, you are coming through victorious.

Day 347

Luke 3:16 John answered, saying unto them all, I indeed baptize you with water; but one mightier than I cometh, the latchet of whose shoes I am not worthy to unloose: he shall baptize you with the Holy Ghost and with fire:

Thought: Don't Be Satisfied With Less Than All

Focus: There Is More Yet To Come

As John, the forerunner of Jesus, taught those that came to be baptized, they asked if he was the Christ. He quickly responded that he was not. The one that is to come was much mightier, while John baptized unto repentance, Jesus would baptize with the Holy Ghost and fire. There was more yet to come.

Your walk with the Lord is a progressive one. With your acknowledgment of who He is, and a desire to follow Him, you were baptized in water. With that wonderful start, prayerfully you continued to receive the Holy Ghost. Even now, as you rejoice having His Spirit, know that there is always a closer walk. Don't be satisfied, continue to press toward the mark.

Day 348

Luke 1:14 And thou shalt have joy and gladness; and many shall rejoice at his birth.

Thought: You Are A Part Of God's Plan To Bless Others

Focus: Remain Humble And Stay Focused On Your Assignment

As Gabriel informed Zacharias that his prayer was heard, he explained that his son would be a blessing to many. He was a part of God's plan. Remaining humble and staying focused on his assignment, he would prepare the way for the coming of the Lord.

Each of God's children are a part of His plan to bless others and to share the message of salvation. As God uses your life in this manner, it is essential that you remain humble and that you stay focused on your assignment. Others are dependent upon you.

Day 349

Luke 1:13 But the angel said unto him, Fear not, Zacharias: for thy prayer is heard; and thy wife Elisabeth shall bear thee a son, and thou shalt call his name John.

Thought: God's Timing Is Perfect

Focus: Fear Not; Your Prayer Has Been Heard

Zacharias and Elizabeth were faithful servants of God. Years earlier they had sought the Lord for a son. Many years later, without that son being born, Zacharias received a visit from Gabriel informing him that his prayer is heard. Elizabeth would give birth to John, who would be the forerunner to Jesus. God's timing was perfect.

God's timing is different from ours. Prayers that you prayed years earlier may appear to have gone unanswered, but in fact they have simply been placed on hold for the proper timing. Do not be overcome with fear, as the Lord informs you that your prayer is heard.

Day 350

Acts 4:16 Saying, What shall we do to these men? for that indeed a notable miracle hath been done by them is manifest to all them that dwell in Jerusalem; and we cannot deny it.

Thought: When God Blesses No One Can Deny It, Not Even Satan

Focus: Let The Story Be Told

The High Priest, and the rulers of the Temple, found themselves in a difficult position. No one, including them, could deny what had been done. A lame man was healed, through the prayers of Peter. As Peter and John continued to declare to all that this miracle came through Jesus, many believed. In the midst of the threats that came, Peter and John continued to teach. The story had to be told.

As God works miracles through your prayers, many will seek to keep others from hearing what has occurred. Do not allow anyone from stopping you from telling what Jesus has done. The story must be told.

Day 351

1 Peter 1:14-15 As obedient children, not fashioning yourselves according to the former lusts in your ignorance: But as he which hath called you is holy, so be ye holy in all manner of conversation;

Thought: Your Past Is Your Past; It Is Time To Live In The Now

Focus: You Have Been Called To Live Holy

Before we had the knowledge of God, our lives were lived seeking to please our flesh. There was no concern for the impact it had on ourselves and others. We now understand the honor of being called by God, which enables us to walk in His will. No matter our assignment, we all have been called to live Holy.

As you look back at your past, you are able to see the many decisions that were made that were not pleasant to God or beneficial to you. God, in His love, called you from that life to a new one. Your past is your past, but you can now enjoy the honor and blessings that God has to offer. You have been called to live holy.

Day 352

Acts 2:2 And suddenly there came a sound from heaven as of a rushing mighty wind, and it filled all the house where they were sitting.

Thought: God Will Make Himself Known

Focus: The Message Needs To Be Heard

As the 120 waited, the scripture informs us that, suddenly, a sound came from heaven and filled the house. God was making Himself heard. Not only would those in the upper room be impacted, but also the multitude of Jews that were in Jerusalem to celebrate Pentecost. All needed to hear the message.

There are messages that the Lord shares with only the individual, but there are also those that are broadcasted to all. As God makes Himself known, it is essential that we listen. The message needs to be heard.

Day 352

Acts 3:8 And he leaping up stood, and walked, and entered with them into the temple, walking, and leaping, and praising God.

Thought: Others Need To Know What God Has Done

Focus: Let Your Praise Be Heard

As Peter took the hand of the man he had prayed for, lifting him up, immediately his bones received strength. The man's immediate response was to begin praising God. He entered the Temple, letting everyone know what God has done. He wanted all to hear his praise.

As the Lord blesses your life, others need to know what has occurred. Let your praise be heard by all. There can be no mistake that it was God who put His hand upon you, in the midst of your need. Let your praise be heard.

Day 353

Genesis 12:1-2 Now the LORD had said unto Abram, Get thee out of thy country, and from thy kindred, and from thy father's house, unto a land that I will shew thee: And I will make of thee a great nation, and I will bless thee, and make thy name great; and thou shalt be a blessing:

Thought: Don't Allow Today To Keep You From Tomorrow

Focus: God Has A Greater Tomorrow Waiting On You

Abram had a comfortable life, one he was thankful for. What he did not know was that God had greater plans for him. That he might receive, a move was required. He had to leave his place of comfort that he might obtain the fullness of God's blessings. He could not allow his today to keep him from his tomorrow.

Abram's move was a natural one, for us a spiritual move is required. Your relationship with God is a good one, but do not allow it to keep you from where God wants to bring you. As you follow His directions, you will enter the place He has determined for you. Don't allow today to keep you from tomorrow.

Day 354

Acts 3:5 And he gave heed unto them, expecting to receive something of them. Then Peter said, Silver and gold have I none; but such as I have give I thee: In the name of Jesus Christ of Nazareth rise up and walk.

Thought: God Has Empowered You To Change Lives

Focus: Someone Is Waiting For You To Speak Into Their Life

As the man begging for alms heard Peter tell him to look at him and John, he anticipated that he would receive something. What he did not know was that it would be more than silver or gold. He was about to be healed. Peter being led by the Spirit, directed the man, in the Name of Jesus, to rise up and walk. He was empowered to change lives.

God has placed His Spirit within you. As you walk in faith with Him, you will discover that He has empowered you to change lives. As you follow the leading of the Lord, He will bring you to those that are waiting for you to speak into their lives. As the Lord directs you, speak, miracles will follow.

Day 355

Acts 2:1 And when the day of Pentecost was fully come, they were all with one accord in one place.

Thought: There Is Power In Oneness

Focus: Proper Focus Is Essential

Some 120 men and women were in one place, seeking one thing; the reception of the promise. Their focus was on what God had told them. They were to wait until they received the power. Their focus was rewarded, the promise was fulfilled. They all received the Holy Ghost.

When a congregation remains focused on the will of God, great things will occur. As you and those that you worship with remain in unity, seeking to obey God, you will experience many signs and wonders, with many being added to the church. There is power in oneness.

Lord, Make us One

Day 356

Acts 2:2 And suddenly there came a sound from heaven as of a rushing mighty wind, and it filled all the house where they were sitting.

Thought for the Day: God Will Make Himself Known

Reflection for the Day: The Message Needs To Be Heard

As the 120 waited, the scripture informs us that, suddenly, a sound came from heaven and filled the house. God was making Himself heard. Not only would those in the upper room be impacted, but also the multitude of Jews that were in Jerusalem to celebrate Pentecost. All needed to hear the message.

There are messages that the Lord shares with only the individual, but there are also those that are broadcast to all. As God makes Himself known, it is essential that we listen. The message needs to be heard.

Day 357

Psalm 100:4-5 Enter into his gates with thanksgiving, and into his courts with praise: be thankful unto him, and bless his name. For the LORD is good; his mercy is everlasting; and his truth endureth to all generations.

Thought: Come Prepared To Praise

Focus: He Has Earned Our Thanksgiving

When we gather for worship, there should be no need for anyone to push us to praise the Lord. We are to enter His gates with thanksgiving and His courts with praise. Surely, He has earned our thanksgiving and deserves our praise.

What is in your spirit when you enter the house of the Lord? Do you enter with praise and a declaration of thanksgiving? You need not have someone to tell you to say thank you or to worship Him. He has earned every praise you can offer Him.

Day 358

Matthew 4:2 And when he had fasted forty days and forty nights, he was afterward an hungred.

Thought: The Enemy Knows Where to Attack You

Focus: Prepare For the Temptations Will Come

The scripture lets us know that the Spirit led Jesus into the wilderness to be tempted by the devil. We also know that the temptation came after he had fasted for forty days and was hungry. The enemy knew where to attack but was not ready for what he discovered. The prayer and fasting had prepared Jesus for the attack. He endured it victoriously.

Each of us has areas in our lives that makes us vulnerable to the attacks of the enemy. What must take place is proper preparation. Stay in God's Word, give yourself to prayer and fasting that when the attack does come, you will be prepared. Start now, don't wait until later.

Day 359

Psalm 95:8 Harden not your heart, as in the provocation, and as in the day of temptation in the wilderness:

Thought: When God Speaks; Respond with Obedience

Focus: Where Others Failed; Succeed

As Israel was led through the wilderness, they chose to ignore the voice of the Lord. As He told them of the "Land of Promise", they responded by murmuring and complaining. Their decision resulted in an entire generation dying in the wilderness.

As God directs your steps, your response is critical. It is essential that the actions you take are ones of obedience. Scripture provides the account of those that chose to murmur and complain, and the result of their decision. When the Lord speaks to you, respond in obedience; victory will follow.

Day 360

Proverbs 15:1 A soft answer turneth away wrath: but grievous words stir up anger.

Thought: Choose Your Words Carefully; They Matter

Focus: You Have the Power To Dilute Strife

The proverb helps us to understand the power of our words. As we choose our words carefully, we can diminish the anger that may exist. If we use the wrong words we will add to the level that already exists. It is essential that we choose our words carefully.

You have been in conversations that have the potential to result in poor decisions being made, because of anger. God has empowered you to diminish that anger. As you choose the proper words, you will be able to turn away from the wrath that is felt. Your words have power.

Day 361

Exodus 18:21 Moreover thou shalt provide out of all the people able men, such as fear God, men of truth, hating covetousness; and place such over them, to be rulers of thousands, and rulers of hundreds, rulers of fifties, and rulers of tens:

Thought: Competency Must Begin With Character

Focus: Truth Is Essential

As Jethro watched his son-in-law Moses judge the people from morning to night, he told him this was not a good thing. He must choose able men to train to assist in this effort. Jethro highlighted they must be men of character, men committed to truth.

Those that lead God's people must be able men and women. It is essential that they be individuals of character, totally committed to the truth of God's Word. Anything less would disqualify them from being in that position. Insist on walking in and sharing truth; it is a must.

Day 362

1 Thessalonians 5:18 In every thing give thanks: for this is the will of God in Christ Jesus concerning you.

Thought: Maintain A Spirit of Thanksgiving

Focus: Circumstances Do Not Control God, God Controls the Circumstances

Our faith in a God that controls all things allows us to maintain a spirit of thanksgiving. We know, regardless of the circumstances, that He remains in total control. Circumstances do not control God; He controls the circumstances.

As you face the various challenges in your life, it is essential that you realize in whom you have placed your trust. Insist on maintaining a spirit of thanksgiving, knowing that the circumstances you are facing do not control God, He controls the circumstances.

Day 363

Romans 6:1-2 What shall we say then? Shall we continue in sin, that grace may abound? God forbid. How shall we, that are dead to sin, live any longer therein?

Thought: Grace Is A Gift; Not A License To Sin

Focus: You Have Died To The Old To Live In The New

The gift of grace must not be understood as freeing the believer to continue in sin. Through baptism, we were buried with Jesus that we might rise up to walk with him. As we thank God for His grace, our commitment is to walk in obedience to His Word and His will.

As you seek to follow the Lord, the need of His grace will remain. Recognizing that this gift is in your life, you must not use it as an excuse to sin. Your focus must be on living a Godly life. You have died to the old, that you might live in the new.

Day 364

1 Peter 5:2 Feed the flock of God which is among you, taking the oversight thereof, not by constraint, but willingly; not for filthy lucre, but of a ready mind;

Thought: Serve Freely; Not For Personal Gain

Focus: Your Assignment Is To Be Completed

Peter is speaking here to the Elders, but the principle shared is applicable to all. Each of us, that has been called to follow Jesus, has an assignment that must be completed. It must be done with a spirit of commitment to the goal, not for personal gain.

You have an assignment that is key to the plan of God. Your willingness to complete it is essential. As you go forth, do so, not for personal gain, but with a ready mind.

Day 365

1 Samuel 30:8 And David enquired at the LORD, saying, Shall I pursue after this troop? shall I overtake them?

Thought: Before Taking Action; Ask For Direction

Focus: God Will Respond

David found himself in the midst of a great storm. Upon returning back to their village, he and his men discovered that the village had been burnt to the ground, with their wives and children taken captive. The men blamed David and spoke of stoning him. How does one respond in such a challenging situation? David's response was to inquire of the Lord for direction. Before taking any action he asked the one that knew; God responded.

In the midst of a storm, emotions can become overwhelming. How one responds at that time is critical. It is essential that you neither accept defeat or rush into action. You must first seek God for direction. Take a moment to encourage yourself and then enquire of the Lord. He will respond.

ABOUT THE AUTHOR

Victor C. Speakman is a multifaceted individual who wears many hats with grace and purpose. As a pastor, singer, and motivational speaker, Victor has dedicated his life to spreading messages of faith, hope, and empowerment to audiences around the world.

With a call to serve others and a deep-rooted faith, Victor C. Speakman has touched countless lives throughout his ministry. As a pastor, he provides spiritual guidance, support, and encouragement to his congregation, helping individuals navigate life's challenges with faith and resilience.

Beyond the pulpit, Victor shares his gift of music with the world. Through soul-stirring melodies and uplifting lyrics, he uses music as a vehicle to inspire, heal, and unite listeners from all walks of life.

As a motivational speaker, Victor C. Speakman empowers audiences with messages of hope, resilience, and personal growth. Through engaging storytelling and powerful insights, he motivates others to overcome obstacles, pursue their dreams, and live life to the fullest with God leading the way.

Victor C. Speakman is passionate about community involvement as shown by his involvement with the DeKalb County NAACP, where he serves as Committee Chair for Criminal Justice. The vision of the NAACP DeKalb is to **EDUCATE** the community about issues that impact our well-being; **EQUIP** us with tools that improve economic success and sustainability; and **EMPOWER** every DeKalb person to exercise their right to be heard.

He is a Motivational/Inspirational Coach and has a passion for people. Victor Speakman has been featured on Fox 5 with Marissa Mitchell regarding his call for an end to youth violence in DeKalb County. Pastor Speakman uses Faith to reach young people and help them live lives of honor. Last, but not least, he is an amazing singer, who has produced his CD. He is also a profound Preacher, who can expound with clarity and confidence on the Word of God.

For more information:

Contact
Victor C. Speakman
Preacher, Speaker, Singer,
Author and Businessman

www.vicspeakman.com

Bethel Original Freewill Baptist Church
1890 Second Avenue
Decatur, GA 30023
www.bethelofwbchurch.org

A Distinct Identity

Mission of BOFW Baptist Church

Outreach and Love

Bethel Original Freewill Baptist Church in Decatur, Georgia is led by Pastor Victor C. Speakman with Lady LaShanta Speakman standing beside him as God leads and directs their paths, knowing that their strength lies not only in the words they stand by, but most importantly through the actions of their initiatives. Working together with our community we believe that we can overcome our challenges much more efficiently as we follow in the steps ordered by our Lord and Savior, Jesus Christ.

NOTES

Made in the USA
Columbia, SC
26 September 2024

42975591R10215